T4-AJU-232

Important Notice

This product is intended for informational use only and is not a substitute for legal advice. State laws vary and change and the information or forms do not necessarily conform to the laws or requirements of your state. While you always have the right to prepare your own documents and to act as your own attorney, do consult an attorney on all important legal matters. You will find a listing of state bar referral services in the Resources section of this product. This product was not prepared by a person licensed to practice law in this state.

Limited warranty and disclaimer

This self-help product is intended to be used by the consumer for his/her own benefit. It may not be reproduced in whole or in part, resold or used for commercial purposes without written permission from the publisher. In addition to copyright violations, the unauthorized reproduction and use of this product to benefit a second party may be considered the unauthorized practice of law.

This product is designed to provide authoritative and accurate information in regard to the subject matter covered. However, the accuracy of the information is not guaranteed, as laws and regulations may change or be subject to differing interpretations. Consequently, you may be responsible for following alternative procedures, or using material or forms different from those supplied with this product. It is strongly advised that you examine the laws of your state before acting upon any of the material contained in this product.

As with any matter, common sense should determine whether you need the assistance of an attorney. We urge you to consult with an attorney, qualified estate planner, or tax professional, or to seek any other relevant expert advice whenever substantial sums of money are involved, you doubt the suitability of the product you have purchased, or if there is anything about the product that you do not understand including its adequacy to protect you. Even if you are completely satisfied with this product, we encourage you to have your attorney review it.

Neither the author, publisher, distributor nor retailer are engaged in rendering legal, accounting or other professional services. Accordingly, the publisher, author, distributor and retailer shall have neither liability nor responsibility to any party for any loss or damage caused or alleged to be caused by the use of this product.

Copyright Notice

The purchaser of this guide is hereby authorized to reproduce in any form or by any means, electronic or mechanical, including photocopying, all forms and documents contained in this guide, provided it is for non-profit, educational or private use. Such reproduction requires no further permission from the publisher and/or payment of any permission fee.

The reproduction of any form or document in any other publication intended for sale is prohibited without the written permission of the publisher. Publication for nonprofit use should provide proper attribution to Made E-Z Products.

Table of contents

How to use this guide

E-Z Legal's Made E-Z™ Guides can help you achieve an important legal objective conveniently, efficiently and economically. But it is important to properly use this guide if you are to avoid later difficulties.

◆ Carefully read all information, warnings and disclaimers concerning the legal forms in this guide. If after thorough examination you decide that you have circumstances that are not covered by the forms in this guide, or you do not feel confident about preparing your own documents, consult an attorney.

◆ Complete each blank on each legal form. Do not skip over inapplicable blanks or lines intended to be completed. If the blank is inapplicable, mark "N/A" or "None" or use a dash. This shows you have not overlooked the item.

◆ Always use pen or type on legal documents—never use pencil.

◆ Avoid erasures and "cross-outs" on final documents. Use photocopies of each document as worksheets, or as final copies. All documents submitted to the court must be printed on one side only.

◆ Correspondence forms may be reproduced on your own letterhead if you prefer.

◆ Whenever legal documents are to be executed by a partnership or corporation, the signatory should designate his or her title.

◆ It is important to remember that on legal contracts or agreements between parties all terms and conditions must be clearly stated. Provisions may not be enforceable unless in writing. All parties to the agreement should receive a copy.

◆ Instructions contained in this guide are for your benefit and protection, so follow them closely.

◆ You will find a glossary of useful terms at the end of this guide. Refer to this glossary if you encounter unfamiliar terms.

◆ Always keep legal documents in a safe place and in a location known to your spouse, family, personal representative or attorney.

Introduction to Buying & Selling A Business Made E-Z™

Buying or selling a business is usually a once-in-a-lifetime experience. For people about to buy or sell a business for the first time, it's a frightening prospect. That's why I wrote *Buying & Selling A Business Made E-Z*. With this guide at their fingertips, a buyer or seller can move ahead intelligently, confidently and successfully on this most important undertaking.

This essential guide steers buyers and sellers through each phase of the buy-sell process. It shows the many proven ways to avoid costly errors, dangerous pitfalls and common mistakes while obtaining the best deal possible. In the following chapters are the proven strategies to:

- plan the acquisition
- position the business for a fast, profitable sale
- find the best opportunities
- investigate and thoroughly evaluate the acquisition
- negotiate the sale on the most favorable terms
- structure the transaction for maximum tax and business benefits
- finance the acquisition
- gain protection with essential, but commonly overlooked contract terms
- ensure a smooth and orderly ownership transfer

Buying & Selling A Business Made E-Z tackles all the troublesome questions and situations a buyer or seller is likely to encounter with clear, step-by-step answers.

Whether planning to buy or sell a small retail shop, a large manufacturing firm, an interest in a franchised company or a turnaround opportunity, this book puts years of experience in acquiring and selling countless businesses right at a buyer's or seller's disposal.

Buying & Selling A Business Made E-Z is not just for buyers and sellers. It also belongs on the desk of accountants, attorneys, business brokers, lenders, appraisers, acquisition consultants and other professionals who can greatly benefit their clients by sharing with them the wealth of information contained in this guide.

This book does more than reveal how to profitably buy or sell a business. It provides the essential tools every buyer and seller needs. As a complete "action kit," this valuable book includes numerous sample forms, checklists, worksheets, sample correspondence, contracts and agreements, and other documents that can save time and money throughout each step of any transfer. A resource-rich companion, this book also lists numerous sources of assistance and references for any buyer or seller requiring more guidance.

Buying or selling a business is always complex because there are invariably many legal, accounting and tax matters to consider. Therefore, no book can, or should, take the place of an attorney or accountant when professional advice for specific situations is needed. But I encourage your advisers to review this book. I'm confident they will recommend it as a most valuable armchair adviser for making those important business decisions.

Arnold S. Goldstein
Deerfield Beach, Florida
July, 1999

Deciding to buy or sell a business

1

Chapter 1

Deciding to buy or sell a business

What you'll find in this chapter:

➡ Who is buying and selling businesses

➡ Five obstacles you may encounter

➡ Starting up a brand new business

➡ Franchises and partnerships

➡ Obtaining professional assistance

About 500,000 businesses now change hands each year. More than 400,000 are small businesses. This statistic does not include:

- transfers between existing stockholders or partners

- transfers within the family or estate transfers

- sales by bankruptcy trustees, receivers, assignees or secured lenders liquidating a distressed business

Many factors influenced this growth in business transfers. One obvious reason is that there are many more businesses in the United States today than ever before. A second reason is the ownership turnover rate. In 1980, the average business remained with the same owner for 12 years. By 1990, the average ownership term was only eight years.

Profiling today's business buyer

More people than ever before want to buy a business. They come from diverse backgrounds and have many different reasons for buying. But unlike buyers of larger businesses, their motives are often more personal than financial. They buy for self-gratification as well as for wealth.

More specific reasons include:

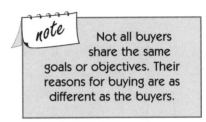

note Not all buyers share the same goals or objectives. Their reasons for buying are as different as the buyers.

◆ There is more income than through employment, or a business may supplement other income.

◆ Business ownership may offer more security than employment. Many buyers are unemployed.

◆ Business ownership lets the buyer engage in more self-satisfying work.

◆ The buyer wants the many tax advantages and fringe benefits available from business ownership.

◆ Ownership may build ego or enhance self-image.

◆ The buyer with an existing business may want economies of scale.

◆ The existing company may want to diversify into new markets, additional product lines or a stronger earnings base.

◆ The acquiring company may be attracted by a seller's cash reserves or undervalued assets.

◆ A company with a cyclical cash flow may want a business to stabilize its cash flow.

◆ The buyer may find a seller's growth prospects more favorable than its own.

◆ A seller may be a valuable source of raw material or exclusive products.

◆ The seller's business may be an outlet for the buyer's products or enhance marketing.

◆ The selling company may have a good management or technical staff.

◆ The selling company may own special processes, inventions or machinery.

◆ The acquisition may feature a valued name or reputation.

> **HINT** Existing companies usually want businesses selling in the $2 million to $20 million range with a positive cash flow and strong growth potential. Middle-market buyers may be large public or private corporations or private investor groups.

◆ An acquisition may be a distressed sale which the buyer may acquire cheap.

Five obstacles to buying a business

Countless people want to buy or start their own business, but only a few do. What holds so many people back? Five major obstacles:

The financial obstacle

Lack of money is the biggest problem. First-time buyers usually overestimate the capital required to buy a particular type and size business. Only by testing the water will the buyer have a fair idea of the cash it will take.

The security obstacle

Buying a business can be frightening because the buyer is leaving behind a steady paycheck. But the intelligent buyer weighs the job security he now has. What if his employer fails or decides to fire him?

The self-confidence obstacle

Prospective buyers may lack the self confidence necessary to buy a business. But the buyer should ask himself why he isn't as capable of running his own business as are the hundreds of thousands of first-time buyers this year—or the millions who run a successful business.

The fear-of-failure obstacle

Buyers do fail. But there is considerably less chance of failure when buying an existing business compared to a new start-up venture. The buyer cannot avoid risk but should know that the potential rewards far outweigh the risks.

The family obstacle

Many buyers are discouraged from fulfilling their ambitions by spouses who resist the idea. A spouse may face many of these obstacles even if the buyer doesn't. If a husband and wife don't share the same goals, failure practically becomes inevitable. The buyer should explain his reasons for wanting the business and try to compromise to resolve concerns. The experience should be a family affair.

The seller's profile

The seller's profile closely follows that of today's buyer. In most instances, the decision to sell comes slowly, and a seller may vacillate for several years before finally deciding to sell. Of course, many buyers have their own false starts, and seldom buy.

The changing times have also changed the seller's profile. Yesterday's small business would only sell because of death, retirement or poor health. The business was the owner's career, and few owners sought alternative opportunities. This is no longer true.

Why are businesses sold?

- The owner dies or is disabled.

- The owner wants to retire.

- The seller's income needs are not satisfied.

note Buyers acquire a business with certain expectations. If those expectations are not quickly realized, they sell.

- The seller is not happy with the business.

- Additional capital is needed by the business which the seller cannot or will not provide.

- The business has had financial problems, and the seller cannot revitalize it.

- A subsidiary is out of balance with the holding company or no longer fits the corporate objectives.

- Cash is needed to liquidate personal debts or to raise revenue for the remaining organization.

- The business becomes too complex, and the seller cannot cope with the new challenges.

- Significant adverse trends or anticipated problems threaten the company's future.

The start-a-business alternative

The decision to buy or start a business must balance many factors. Some types of businesses are best started from scratch. These ventures usually feature unique products or services. The choice between buying and starting becomes more difficult for common businesses, such as a hardware store or a travel agency. Entrepreneurial instincts may be decisive. Many are excited by the challenge of building a new business from the ground floor. Others prefer an operating business. They can operate a business but not muster what it takes to build a business from thin air.

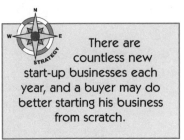

There are countless new start-up businesses each year, and a buyer may do better starting his business from scratch.

Additional factors influence the start-up alternative:

- ◆ *The acquired business has a track record.* The buyer knows its sales and profits. A start-up is sheer speculation. The acquired business is ordinarily a safer investment because its performance is more predictable.

- ◆ *Buying a business is easier.* Customers, employees, suppliers and the physical plant are in place. It takes considerable effort to launch a start-up.

- ◆ *The buyer can more easily finance an acquisition.* The existing business has a track record, available collateral to pledge, the possibility of seller financing or other financing opportunities that are unavailable with a start-up.

- ◆ *A start-up may be less expensive.* The buyer need not pay for a seller's goodwill. But a start-up may lose considerable money before reaching break-even, and be more costly in the long run than a profitable acquisition with a higher price tag.

♦ The one major advantage of a start-up? *The buyer creates precisely the business he wants.* Size, layout, merchandising, image and location are as he wants it.

The franchise factor

Assuming a solid business franchise is available, the buyer must consider both its advantages and disadvantages. The major advantage? A franchise reduces the risk of failure. The failure rate of franchised businesses is under five percent compared with the 50 percent for independent businesses.

> **HOT spot** With over 2,000 franchise systems in the United States, franchised operations generate close to 50 percent of all retail sales.

To help ensure the buyer's success is the franchiser's training, assistance, supervision and a blueprint to successfully operate the business. Franchiser assistance and reduced risk is an important benefit for buyers who lack managerial experience or confidence operating their own independent business. The franchised business has a recognized name for higher sales and profits.

On the other hand, a good franchised business is usually more expensive. The more successful franchise—such as McDonald's—sells for several times the price of a comparable independent business. There are also continuing royalty payments of two to four percent. So buying a franchise can be costly. Still, a franchise may be cost-justified by its higher sales and profits.

The franchise buyer may feel more like an employee than a boss. When purchasing a franchise, the buyer adopts the company's name, layout, merchandising, pricing and operating policies and operates by the franchiser's strict rules. While this is an advantage for those who welcome close managerial support, a franchise is not for the entrepreneurial individual who wants to run the business his own way without franchiser constraints.

The partnership question

Another question for the buyer is whether he should take a partner or journey into business alone. The buyer might consider this as he would the franchise question, because a franchise is very similar to a partnership.

A partner may provide the confidence and psychological support needed to take the entrepreneurial plunge. Good partnerships create a synergy where far more is accomplished together. A partner's capital also can be important. More funding allows the buyer to build the business faster.

Partnership success depends chiefly on the partners' ability to get along and develop a good working relationship. This remains the one big drawback of a partnership. It is difficult to avoid conflict when partners work closely together. A partnership also financially strains the smaller business as a "two-paycheck" business.

> The right partner, properly selected to balance the buyer's management skills and interests, can strengthen overall management.

So, is a partnership a good or a bad idea? A partner is right only if the buyer is confident he has found the individual he can totally trust, has complete confidence in, enjoys working with and shares a vision with for the future business.

Finding the right professional assistance

Both the buyer and seller need experienced accountants and attorneys to safely guide them through the buy-sell process.

The lawyer's role

The attorney must have skill, diligence and competence in many different areas of law.

- **Contract Law.** To safeguard the client's interests with the most effective agreements possible.

- **Taxation.** To structure the transaction with the least adverse tax consequence.

- **Secured Transaction.** To protect a seller extending financing to the buyer.

- **Leases.** To insure the buyer proper leases and tenancies.

> **HOT** spot Transferring a larger firm may also present SEC, antitrust and other considerations requiring specialized representation.

- **Corporate and Partnership Law.** To handle the divergent interests of stockholders and partners within the buyer or seller organization.

- **Debtor-Creditor Rights.** To safeguard the assets being acquired from creditor claims.

- **Bankruptcy.** Because many insolvent firms are acquired through insolvency proceedings, counsel must have a thorough knowledge of insolvency law and procedure.

- **Franchising.** To handle the special transfer problems imposed on more than 40 percent of all retail and service businesses operating as a franchise.

- **Financing.** To help the client take advantage of the new trends of leveraged buyouts, venture capital and governmental funding programs.

The accountant's role

The accountant's role is as important as the attorney's. Many acquisitions are financially faulty. The client without sound financial and accounting guidance has no way to economically evaluate the transaction.

The accountant has two major functions. First, the accountant must help evaluate the business. Second, the accountant should tax plan for the transaction. The accountant must objectively determine if the acquisition can produce earnings and discharge its financing.

The small business consultant

Few new entrepreneurs use business consultants. A consultant can help clear this entrepreneurial minefield. The fees run from expensive to free; SBA's (SCORE) group gives free help.

How to sell quickly and for top price

2

Chapter 2

How to sell quickly and for top price

The decision to sell

Many owners are blind to the need to sell. The hopelessly mismanaged business is headed for failure, or the owner plans to turn the business over to a son or daughter of questionable competence. Or, a business can never achieve the owner's financial goals.

More commonly, the owner sells because alternatives have not been considered. Or consider the financially troubled business. For the owner unable to achieve his own turnaround, a sale is probably appropriate.

Partnership disputes are another common reason for selling. When the dispute cannot be resolved, the wiser alternative is to transfer ownership to one partner rather than sell the entire business to a third party.

The threat of serious competition, the loss of a major customer or another sudden crisis rushes many sellers into a too hasty sale. Once the business is sold, the seller may look back with regret. The gains from a sale must be weighed against what will be forfeited. The owner may not realize the value of the many perks and other hidden benefits or have unreasonable expectations about what the business will sell for.

Resolving internal problems

Conflicts within the business are a frequent obstacle to an advantageous sale. If partners are involved, opinions are seldom unanimous on whether or not the business should be sold, and there may be disagreement about price, terms and timing.

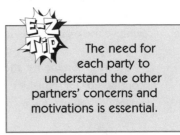

Few partners agree on all issues. Invariably, each partner views the business from his own perspective. One partner may see the business as a needed source of income; another may consider it a poor investment. One partner may work 40-hour weeks and the other partner 10 hours. The family-owned business has its own conflicts. Even when owned by one family member, the pressure to sell—or not to sell—may be considerable.

The lawyer or accountant can help resolve internal conflicts. In many cases, resolution may be reached by communication between the parties.

When agreement cannot be reached on a sale—or its terms—there should be a buy-out arrangement within the partnership. The most workable solution is to give the dissenting partner the right of first refusal to buy at a price offered by a third party and acceptable to the partner anxious to sell.

The need for each party to understand the other partners' concerns and motivations is essential.

Owners holding a controlling interest in the business must protect themselves against derivative stockholder suits from dissenting minority stockholders. Minority stockholders may restrain the sale or rescind a completed transaction. Specific procedures to protect majority stockholders against dissenting minority stockholders include:

+ A review of the corporate bylaws and state corporation laws to determine whether the selling stockholder holds or controls the requisite stock interest.

+ Advising minority stockholders of the intended sale. Full and open disclosure is vital to dissuade any stockholder claim of a bad faith sale.

+ Hold formal stockholder and director meetings before signing any sales agreement, unless the agreement provides that obtaining the requisite stockholder vote is a subsequent condition.

+ An independent appraisal of the business can show the sale is for a fair and reasonable price. Documenting a fair price is essential to bar a minority stockholder's claim of breach of fiduciary duty or fraudulent transfer.

Financially positioning the business

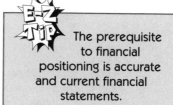

The prerequisite to financial positioning is accurate and current financial statements.

Before marketing the business for sale, the seller and his accountant must financially position the business. Small businesses keep notoriously poor financial records and many businesses remain unsold, or are sold for far less than their true value because the buyer could not estimate performance from the seller's scant financial records. Some sellers see sparse records as a blessing when their objective is to conceal losses. Buyers may assume losses are more than reflected and offer less for the business.

Financial positioning:

1) favorably presents the business

> **note**
> Buyers will expect to review income statements, tax returns, balance sheets, and cash flow statements for three to five years.

2) identifies changes in the financial structure to best position the business for sale

3) projects (for the buyer) the business's future profitability and cash flow

Maximizing the profit potential

For buyers, the income statement is most important because historical profits greatly predict future profitability. Many enterprises are profitable but do not show profits. To avoid taxes, they fail to report income, take extraordinary write-offs, accelerate depreciation and create other "paper" expenses. With poor profits, the seller must expect a poor price.

Timing the sale is part of financial positioning. While it is not always possible to anticipate a sale two or three years in advance, you may delay a sale until the financial statements can show maximum profits. Quarterly statements can reflect maximum profits from when the decision to sell the business is made.

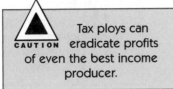

> **CAUTION** Tax ploys can eradicate profits of even the best income producer.

The seller's accountant should highlight extraordinary expenses that lowered the profits. A simple financial reconstruction may turn heavy paper losses into substantial earnings —highlighting true operational profitability.

The seller must give the buyer reasons for diminished profits, particularly factors unlikely to be encountered by the buyer. Small-business buyers can rarely reconstruct the profitability of a business under their own management. Reconstructed statements must accompany the actual financial statements or tax returns.

note

Small business buyers are primarily interested in profits. The business may appear unprofitable, while its owners may be taking substantial incomes and perks from the business. To emphasize the financial benefits to the owner, the seller needs a supplemental statement reflecting the owners' salaries, fringe benefits, perks, pensions, business-owned automobiles, travel, wages to other family members, and the numerous other personal perks charged against the business.

HOT spot Buyers are most interested in current sales because buyers may believe the business is for sale because of recent problems or reduced sales.

The seller must anticipate buyer questions about the business' profitability. The seller may have to explain discrepancies between the financial statements and tax returns as well as chronic losses, adverse trends or other negatives that diminish value.

Positioning the balance sheet

A second objective is to adjust the assets and liabilities of the business for a faster and smoother sale. Before marketing the business, the balance sheet should be made as lean as possible.

1) **Reduce inventory** to the lowest possible operational level to create cash flow and reduce the price, making it far easier to sell, assuming the seller will retain cash proceeds.

2) **Turn delinquent receivables over for collection.**

3) **Sell excess or unused capital assets** such as equipment, furniture or fixtures, which have no value to the buyer.

4) **Reduce current liabilities and accounts payable.** Some sellers prefer to offer the business for sale without debt; however, this may be a mistake. Allowing the buyer to assume liabilities may help finance the sale and reduce the buyer's down-payment.

5) **Review stockholder loans.** Loans due to or from owners or officers of the business should be repaid unless there are serious tax implications.

6) **Pay tax liabilities, delinquent expenses and overdue accounts**—always negatively magnified by buyers.

Projecting a bright financial future

Buyers buy the business' future. The past is important only to help project that future. Sellers must provide the buyer a clear, optimistic vision of the business and put the business in the best possible light.

Are sales increasing? Use a sales graph. Another graph can show increasing profits and other favorable financial trends. Outline every factor, indicator and trend that emphasizes potential for future sales and profits.

note Financial statements have little value when the buyer cannot easily use them to project ahead.

Combine cash flow projections with the income statement to help the buyer estimate how much financing the business can support and operating capital the buyer will need.

Legal positioning

Legal positioning:

- clears any legal impediments to a sale

- attends to legal matters necessary for an orderly business transfer

Sellers often bring a sale to the point of consummation only to find legal impediments. The seller's counsel should identify and remove such corporate, contractual, financial and legal impediments.

+ Does the seller have the legal authority to sell? For the business with partners or multiple stockholders, does the selling stockholder control the votes necessary to sell?

+ Is the business owned by an estate? Have all probate requirements been satisfied? If the sale requires court approval, the sale should be conditional upon court approval.

CAUTION

+ Is the business franchised? A franchised business cannot ordinarily be sold without franchiser approval. Conditions of assignment and buyer criteria must be investigated.

+ What contracts can interfere with a sale? Are key production or distributorship agreements assignable?

+ Is a satisfactory lease available? Review proposed terms of a new lease before marketing the business.

✦ Is the business solvent? Unless the price can fully satisfy creditor claims, determine whether creditors will settle for less payment or whether reorganization or other debtor's remedies to reduce debt will be needed.

The pre-sale legal checklist

The legal review depends upon the nature of the business, legal problems, assets to be sold, and the transaction's structure. Also review:

- *Pending litigation* and its impact on any proposed sale.

- *Employment contracts* to determine whether they can be assigned or terminated without penalty.

- *Union contracts* and their assignability.

- *Employee pension plans and profit-sharing* and their assignability or provisions for termination.

- *Existing contracts* and their assignability or rights to terminate.

- *Secured loans, conditional sales agreements and equipment leases* to determine their current status and rights to assign or terminate.

- *Patents, trademarks and licenses* to determine whether they are properly filed.

- *Corporate records* to verify required filings and that the corporate minute book is current.

- *Obligations between the owners and the corporation* to determine conditions of termination.

- *Personal guarantees* by owners of the corporation to creditors and their rights to terminate.

Establishing the sale terms

The seller must market the business at the price he expects and establish other key terms of sale. A sale's plan must be:

- **Comprehensive.** It must cover all essential terms of sale, not only the price.

- **Objective.** The seller must set realistic and objective terms.

- **Flexible.** The seller must know the minimally acceptable terms. The seller must also know the trade-offs and negotiable points.

With these points in mind, the sales plan must answer these questions:

- ◆ *Assets to be sold.* Which assets will be sold, and which will the seller retain?

  - cash on hand

  - accounts receivable

  - note(s) receivable

  - prepaid deposits

  - inventory

  - furniture and fixtures

  - equipment

  - automobiles and motor vehicles

  - leasehold improvements

  - patents, trademarks and copyrights

  - customer lists

- name and goodwill
- contract rights
- assignment of lease
- telephone numbers
- real estate

◆ *Price.*

- What is the asking price for the business?
- Is the price firm or negotiable?
- If the price is negotiable, what is the "bottom" price?
- Will the price be adjusted to actual asset values (inventory, receivables)?
- Is the price exclusive or inclusive of liabilities? If liabilities are to be assumed by the buyer, what amount of liability is the price based upon? Will the price be adjusted to the actual debts?
- Is the price a "net price" after payment of brokerage fees?

◆ *Financing.* Does the seller require an all-cash sale or is seller financing available? If seller financing is available:

- What "down payment" is required?
- What interest rate and re-payment plan are offered?
- What collateral is required?
- Can the buyer assume existing debts toward the purchase price?

◆ *Types of transfer.* Does the seller contemplate a sale of:

- Assets?
- Corporate shares?

- A merger? Will the seller accept shares of stock for the purchase price?

♦ *Leases and Tenancies.*

  - Is a lease available?

  - What are the rent terms, length of tenancy, and other lease terms?

  - If the seller is the lesser, will the buyer have an option or right of first refusal to buy the real estate? If an option is available, what is the option price and option period?

♦ *Employment.* Do principals or other key personnel of the business require employment with the buyer as a condition of the sale? If so:

  - What is the general job description?

  - Required salary?

  - If employment is required, on what terms?

  - Will the seller assist the buyer for a period after the sale?

  - Will other key personnel remain with the business after the sale?

♦ *Noncompete Agreement.* Will the principals or other key personnel agree not to compete with the buyer? If so:

  - What activities will the seller not engage in?

  - What geographic area and time period will the non-compete agreement cover?

♦ *Closing Dates.* Does the seller have any preference or requirements for a closing date?

Preparing the offering circular

The offering circular is usually prepared by the business broker, however, a seller may easily prepare his own to assist brokers or to directly deal with potential buyers. The offering circular should give the buyer enough information to determine whether or not the business warrants further investigation. It should include:

- a brief narrative of the origin and history of the company

- the number of years established and/or under the same ownership

- a description of the business' primary products and markets

- general location of the business

- annual sales

- pretax profits (if profitable)

- asking price

- the broker or person to contact

Definition:

Offering circular. This document highlights the key characteristics about the business, its history, and the basic terms of sale.

Working with business brokers

Business brokers sell about 60 percent of all small businesses. Many sellers question whether they should try to sell the business on their own before listing the business with a broker. There is no one right answer. However, it is probably best to approach industry sources first. Good businesses are usually sold quickly by spreading the word within their industry network. If the business cannot be sold within 60-90 days, consider brokers. A longer delay only makes the business shopworn and less interesting even to brokers.

The right broker can help in every phase of the sale—from valuation to arranging financing. How does a seller select the right broker? Only a few states now require licensure. The industry still has many brokers with neither the capability nor expertise to market businesses effectively. Listing the business with an ineffective broker needlessly delays the sale.

> **HINT** Sellers usually see the broker's role as only to find a buyer. While this is their primary mission, professional brokers offer more.

When selecting a broker consider five points:

1) *Is the firm established?* A broker should be established for at least three years.

2) *Is the broker active?* Are there affiliated offices? Employed broker-salespeople? Do they actively advertise other businesses?

3) *Does the broker specialize in this type business?* This can be a big advantage. There are brokerage firms that specialize only in restaurants, bars, nursing homes, drug stores and motels. Because they are familiar with the industry, the specialized broker is exceptionally qualified to determine a fair price, evaluate the business and quickly locate buyers from within the industry.

4) *Has the broker thoroughly evaluated the business?* Has he recommended ways to position the business for sale? This is the most important test.

Understanding brokerage agreements

There are three types of brokerage agreements:

1) **Open listings.** These allow the seller to sell the business either directly or through other brokers. The broker only gets a commission if he finds the buyer. Because the broker competes with the seller and other brokers, he has less incentive to actively market the business. Few brokers accept open listings.

2) **Exclusive agency.** An exclusive agency allows the seller to sell on his own, but not through another broker. Most sellers find this most advantageous, and most brokers accept it.

3) **Exclusive brokerage.** Also called an "exclusive right to sell," this allows the broker a commission whether or not he sells the business, or whether sold through another broker or by the seller. This type listing justifies heavy advertising on the listing.

Five more brokerage agreement provisions

The type listing frames the brokerage arrangement but the seller must also consider five additional points:

1) Commission

The commission and allowed expenses should be in writing together with other contractual terms, including services and expenses to be

> *note* Most brokers charge a $5,000 to $10,000 minimum commission.

provided by the broker. Broker commissions for the smaller business are typically 10 percent of the final sales price, but commissions vary. Some brokers adopt a sliding commission decreasing as the sales price increases.

Larger companies that sell for over $1 million may base the commission on the so-called Lehman formula, which is five percent on the first $1 million, reduced by one percent for each $1 million in sales price thereafter.

Negotiating too low a commission may be counter-productive. Brokers who work on reduced commission frequently devote more effort to their full commission listings.

With a net-price listing, the broker gets any amount over a stipulated net price. If the broker accepts a net price listing, he may believe either the business is underpriced or that the broker can later renegotiate. Net-price listings are seldom equitable to sellers and brokers.

2) Payment of commissions

The agreement also should clarify how commissions will be computed. For example, if the seller sells his shares of corporate stock for $50,000 and the buyer assumes $200,000 in debts, will the commission be based on the full sales price of $250,000 or the $50,000 net to the seller? Brokerage agreements don't always spell this out clearly. Commissions should also be payable only upon the buyer closing the transaction. If there is a breach by the buyer, the seller and broker should share the deposit.

3) Seller's approval

If the seller offers financing—or if the seller retains a residual or contingent liability under the sale requiring a creditworthy buyer, the brokerage agreement should give the seller the right to reject an unqualified buyer without liability for a commission.

4) Brokerage term

Exclusive brokerage listings should give the broker sufficient time to find buyers. A 90-day listing with extensions if the broker is generating reasonable buyer activity is typical.

5) Brokerage disclosures

The seller should give the broker all information needed to market the business. This includes all prior marketing efforts, as well as prior offers and the names of prospective buyers who have shown interest.

The seller should advise the broker about information to be kept confidential.

Sellers should also disclose problems with the business and their reasons so the broker can be prepared for buyer comments.

A seller should never let the broker know the minimum acceptable price as the broker may then offer the business at this lower price to achieve a faster sale. Similarly, other possible concessions (such as financing) should be left for negotiation.

How to evaluate any business

3

Chapter 3

How to evaluate any business

Targeting the ideal business

Before beginning the search, the buyer should prepare a "business profile" of the target acquisition outlining five points:

1) *The type business.* What type business is preferred? What specific characteristics are important? Is the description too restrictive or too broad? Why does the buyer want this type business? Will the buyer enjoy this business? Can the buyer effectively manage it? What background, experience or training does the buyer bring to this business? Will this business satisfy the buyer's objectives?

2) *Geography.* Within what geographic area should the business be located? Can the business readily be found within this area or should the business criteria or geographic area be expanded?

3) *Size.* What approximate sales volume or size business is wanted? Can the buyer manage this size business or should he start with a smaller first venture? Can a business of the desired size generate sufficient income? Can the buyer afford this size business?

4) *Financial Condition.* Does the buyer prefer a turnaround or a stable, well-performing business? If a turnaround or distressed business is preferred, does the buyer have the managerial capability and financial resources to achieve the turnaround?

5) *Down Payment.* Can the target business be acquired with the buyer's available cash?

An appropriate acquisition must always pass a four-part test:

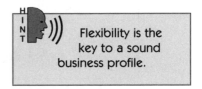

Flexibility is the key to a sound business profile.

1) the buyer can enjoy the business

2) the buyer can manage the business

3) the buyer can earn sufficient income from the business

4) the buyer can afford the business

Many buyers search too rigidly for their ideal business and quickly become disillusioned when no such business is found. Buyers must enter the market with a clear idea of the business they are looking for, yet open to modifying their requirements once they investigate a number of opportunities and gained a better sense of the marketplace.

Finding opportunities

Buyers can investigate too few opportunities. Only when a buyer investigates many opportunities can he compare and determine relative values. A well-conducted search will expose the buyer to scores of possibilities over several months. To sharpen his judgment, the buyer should also probe opportunities that do not fit his criteria. The effort may not result in an acquisition, but it will give the buyer more confidence and sharper ability to evaluate possible acquisitions closer to his criteria.

A productive search requires sufficient leads. The buyer should contact as many potential sources as possible. Industry and trade association referrals

Newspaper listings may produce better leads than brokers can.

are the best starting point, bringing the best results and identifying businesses not yet actively marketed through brokers or newspapers. Many newspaper classifieds list unsaleable businesses, yet sellers often advertise before listing with a broker.

Business brokers are the most common source of business opportunities. However, a buyer cannot rely only on one or even a few brokers. A buyer must make as many broker contacts as possible. Business buyers seldom directly solicit prospective businesses, but this can be one of the best strategies to finding good opportunities—although it is the most expensive and time-consuming.

Mail-inquiries to potential acquisitions can be effective for buyers. Even more effective is telemarketing, which can canvass hundreds of businesses within a target industry and produce many leads never advertised or listed for sale. Supplier leads are also good. Vendors know customers ready to sell and they can provide leads long before the business is actively marketed. Suppliers will expect the buyer's future business should an acquisition result, which should be confirmed beforehand.

Direct mail and supplier leads are both effective because they bring the buyer in contact with businesses before competing buyers even know the business is for sale. Good businesses are almost always sold by word-of-mouth via the industry network. Those that require extensive advertising or brokers are typically overpriced or have other serious problems. This does not mean the shopworn business may not be a worthwhile acquisition. Sellers may market their business at an inflated price, and lower their price only after it remains unsold. Or, the business may have qualities or possibilities overlooked by other buyers.

Follow-up is as important as the number and diversity of sources. The business not for sale today may be on the market next month.

The successful search not only seeks new leads, but follows-up on prior possibilities.

The preliminary evaluation

The preliminary evaluation helps the buyer to quickly screen potential acquisitions. The evaluation never proceeds in distinct stages but evolves on several fronts until either the buyer decides the business no longer warrants consideration—or is finally acquired.

The preliminary evaluation does not always allow the buyer to objectively determine whether or not the business can meet his criteria, or whether the business can be transformed into one that can fulfill his objectives.

Sales is one example. A buyer may seek a business with sales over $500,000 annually, but should this eliminate the $400,000 business with the potential to gross $500,000? Does this $400,000 business generate higher profits than a $500,000 business? To answer these questions requires more than a cursory look at the business.

The seller's demands may create another artificial roadblock during the preliminary evaluation. For example, a seller may ask $100,000 for a business the buyer quickly values at $50,000. The inexperienced buyer may lose the business to a more experienced buyer, who realizes the asking price and terms should never disqualify a deal but are matters for negotiation

Qualifying the acquisition depends on positive answers to four key questions:

1) Is the location or geographic area acceptable?

2) Can the business produce the profits the buyer wants?

3) Can the business be made into the type the buyer wants?

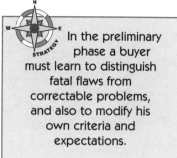

In the preliminary phase a buyer must learn to distinguish fatal flaws from correctable problems, and also to modify his own criteria and expectations.

4) Is there an acceptable lease on the premises?

The business evaluation checklist

The checklist below details information a buyer must ask about the business to help the buyer detect commonly overlooked problems.

The business evaluation must establish the suitability of the acquisition from a business standpoint. However, many of the investigated items and the problems encountered will again require attention in the final negotiation of the transaction as well as when preparing the sales agreement. This underscores again the importance of good coordination between the buyer and his attorney and accountant.

The specific investigation checklist, of course, depends on the type business, age of the company, financial condition and the reported or suspected reason for sale.

Product/Service Analysis

• Obtain description of each product line.

• What is the relative importance of each product/service?

- What is the market share for each product/service?

- What are the growth trends for each product/service?

- What is the anticipated longevity or life cycle for each product/service?

- Who are the principal competitors for each product/service?

- What market share is held by each competitor?

- Are the product lines complete or are additional products needed?

- Are the seller's products/services licensed or subject to license rights?

- What new product planning is underway by the seller?

- How stable is each product/service?

Customer Analysis

- Who are the major customers?

- What sales come from each major customer?

- What percentage of sales comes from each major customer?

- How long has the seller sold to each major customer?

- Are customers under contract, and if so, what are the contract terms?

- Are the customers likely to remain with a new buyer?

- What sales come from foreign customers? Government or military customers?

- How financially stable is each major customer?

- Is repeat business increasing or decreasing?

- Does the repeat business compare favorably to industry averages?

- Is there evidence of a recent or threatened loss of a major customer?

- What are the pending orders? Future orders?

Sales Analysis

- How are the seller's products marketed?

- What sales come from each sales or marketing method?

- Is the sales force organized well and can it handle the present business?

- Do sales and marketing costs compare favorably to industry averages?

- Does the selling organization perform cost effectively in relation to sales?

- Are sales personnel on salary or commission?

- Does the sales compensation plan provide sufficient motivation?

- Are territories allocated properly or are new sales territories needed?

- Is the sales effort supported adequately by advertising?

- What changes in sales strategy are needed to handle new products? New markets? Achieve projected sales?

Advertising Analysis

- Does the seller have a planned advertising and promotional program?

- Does the advertising program feature institutional or product advertising, or both? Is the advertising mix appropriate?

- How does the seller's advertising costs compare to industry averages?

- What are the advertising costs for each product line?

- Is advertising handled internally or by an outside agency, or both?

- Is an advertising agency under contract?

- For what period has the advertising agency represented the company?

- Is additional advertising required to build sales to an acceptable level?

- Are extraordinary expenses required to launch new products?

- What advertising changes will the buyer need and at what additional cost?

Management Analysis

- Does an organizational chart delineate clear management functions?

- Are the lines of authority and responsibility well defined?

- Is the organizational structure appropriate for the size and type business?

- What organizational changes must a buyer initiate?

- Is management understaffed or overstaffed?

- Is management rated on performance?

- Are key managers under contract, and if so, on what terms?

- Have key personnel signed noncompete agreements?

Employee Analysis

- Is the company union or non-union?

- Is there a threat of future unionization or prior collective bargaining attempts?

- Is this type of business or industry typically unionized?

- Would a unionization effort succeed?

- What is the compensation structure?

- Are wages competitive within the industry? The market?

- What percentage of employees are highly skilled?

- Can replacement or additional personnel be readily obtained?

- Can the number of employees be readily altered to meet production or sales needs?

- How do working conditions compare to industry standards?

- Is there an apprenticeship or training program for new employees?

- What are the personnel policies and procedures?

- Does employee turnover compare favorably to industry standards?

- What employee changes will be required?

Research and Development Analysis

- What research and development is on-going?

- How much research and development is spent on each major product or line?

- What are the short- and long-term research and development objectives?

- How much is spent on research and development? How do these costs compare to product revenues? Industry standards?

- What projects under R&D are most promising?

- How many employees are in R&D? How are they divided between supervisory, technical and non-technical personnel?

- How productive is R&D in developing successful new products?

- What is the company's reputation for developing innovative new products?

Market and Competitive Analysis

- What are the demographics of the seller's market?

- Is the market growing, stable or declining?

- Does the market now exist or is it emerging?

- What market share is the seller's? Is the seller's market share growing or declining?

- What internal and external factors will control future market share?

- Who are the major competitors?

- What are the company's competitive strengths and weaknesses?

- What future competitive changes are foreseeable?

- What legal factors may influence product demand or the seller's competitive advantage?

- What changes are needed to maintain market share and a strong competitive position?

- What are the company's short- and long-term growth prospects?

- What expenditures are required to achieve this growth?

Facility Analysis

- Is the location stable?

- Does the plant have adequate space for its present needs?

- Can the plant be expanded for future growth?

- What renovations or improvements are required to improve efficiency?

- Is the plant adequately served by public utilities? Transportation? Shipping?

Lease Analysis

- Are the facilities leased or owned by the seller? If owned, is the property included in the sale?

- Can the building be sold and leased back?

- Will the lease be of sufficient duration to justify the investment?

- Can the business be readily relocated at a reasonable cost?

- Does the proposed lease have a reasonable rent?

Material and Equipment Analysis

- Obtain a complete list of equipment, machinery, furniture and fixtures.

- What is the appraised value of the equipment?

- Is the equipment owned or leased? If leased, on what terms? Can the equipment lease be assumed by a buyer?

- Is the equipment in good working order?

- Are the plant and equipment adaptable to other uses?

- Is new equipment required? If so, at what cost?

Inventory and Purchasing Analysis

- Obtain a list of the company's present and past suppliers.

- How long have the vendors done business with the company?

- Are vendor relations satisfactory?

- Are alternative suppliers available? Will they sell on equally advantageous terms?

- Does the company depend on one supplier? If so, is continued supply assured?

- Are any suppliers related to the seller?

- Do supplier prices compare favorably to competitors' prices?

- Are purchasing procedures well organized and functioning properly?

- Does the company buy advantageously?

- Does the company have good credit?

- Is the company bound to purchasing requirements or vendor contracts?

- Are inventories adequate, overstocked or depleted?

- Is the inventory mix appropriate?

- What additional inventories are required?

- What inventory is shopworn, obsolete or unsaleable?

Confidentiality and due diligence

A buyer cannot rely solely upon the seller's records, plant inspections or representations by principals of the selling company. The buyer must use outside sources to confirm and verify every aspect of the seller's operation and confer with employees, customers, suppliers and other sources who have a different relationship with the company. Outside sources report strengths and weaknesses more objectively than internal sources.

HINT: The seller and buyer must adopt a balanced approach, since breach of confidentiality can destroy a sale.

Two problems may prevent the buyer from approaching external sources. The seller may want to keep a pending sale confidential and not allow a prospective buyer to disclose the possibility of a sale with these parties. Also, these parties may have allegiance to the seller and not candidly expose problems.

The buyer should have the opportunity to confer with at least some outside sources. Whether the seller allows outside interviews depends on how far along the transaction is, whether these sources know that the business is on the market, and whether disclosure would adversely affect their relationship with the business.

Seller selection only allows the seller to choose those who will issue the most favorable reports. Instead, the buyer and seller should randomly select sources. Once selected, the seller should encourage these sources to meet privately with the prospective buyer for a confidential, candid interview.

Employees and suppliers are least likely to be negative about the company for fear of seller retaliation if the sale fails. Employees, particularly top managers, may be overly critical to impress a prospective buyer (and a possible new employer).

> **note** The objectivity of the obtained information requires the buyer to objectively assess those providing it.

The one best way to evaluate a business is for the buyer to work within the business for a reasonable time. Again, sellers resist this for fear of disclosing the business is for sale; however, the purpose of the buyer's involvement can usually be concealed from employees. From this vantage point the buyer can best detect the personalities, peculiarities, and idiosyncrasies of the business as well as the problems, strengths and weaknesses that a business reveals only to those who get truly close to it.

Sellers are also equally as concerned about disclosing any confidential information and trade secrets, which would be detrimental if used for an improper purpose. Before the business is marketed, the seller and his counsel should identify the information that is confidential trade secrets, and when they will disclose this sensitive information to prospective buyers and on what conditions.

Before disclosing trade secrets and other highly confidential or proprietary information, the seller should:

- thoroughly check the prospective buyer and his past and present affiliations for potential security problems.

- require the buyer to execute a confidentiality and non-disclosure agreement.

The confidentiality agreement should require the prospective buyer to hold the information confidential with no unapproved use by the buyer and for indemnification arising from any breach.

Unless the seller has a long lease, a prospective buyer should agree not to lease on the property, unless as part of acquiring the business. Still, enforcement is difficult because the buyer may conceal his affiliation with any new corporate tenant.

Interpreting the results

Every company has advantages and disadvantages, strengths and weaknesses. Blending these into a final decision to buy or not buy is the heart of the acquisition process.

An experienced, confident buyer may decide this alone. The accountant's financial and lawyer's legal evaluation then only support and corroborate the facts and premises upon which the buyer makes the acquisition decision. However, buyers lacking broad industry experience are usually ill-equipped to evaluate a business on their own. Their accountant and attorney can offer little assistance in the business or operational areas, so there is a lack of business expertise needed to evaluate the company as a business.

note No matter how carefully a buyer screens an acquisition, the decision to buy usually rests mostly on entrepreneurial instinct.

A consultant can then assist in the evaluation. Unfortunately, too few buyers utilize consultants to help compensate for their own inexperience in areas where serious problems may exist and be overlooked.

As every seasoned business person can attest, no buyer buys on the strength of objective, quantitative standards alone. Invariably the buyer must rely on a sixth sense.

The financial investiga-tion

4

Chapter 4

The financial investigation

A thorough financial investigation is vital. Numerous acquisitions fail, with considerable loss to their buyers, because the investigation never uncovered significant financial flaws or revealed that the business could never make economic sense.

The financial investigation must:

1) Verify that the financial affairs are as represented.

2) Project the future profitability of the business to the buyer. Only when both conditions are satisfied does the acquisition pass the financial test.

Beyond the financial statements

Perplexing for business buyers and their accountants is the accuracy of the seller's financial records, particularly with a small business. Without accurate records, the buyer's accountant cannot verify the financial history of the enterprise or accurately forecast future performance under a buyer's management.

> **HOT spot** If the seller is to finance the sale, he must be as concerned as the buyer about whether the business can pay the loan.

There are many reasons for poor financial records. Small business operators ignore their managerial importance and operate their businesses through instinct. Often, no adequate accounting system is used, nor is it unusual to find businesses without financial statements, or with tax returns that are two or three years delinquent.

The accuracy of financial statements is generally suspect. Few businesses have certified statements, for unlike large businesses, they are not public corporations and do not require certified statements. Their financial statements are then usually an unaudited patchwork of numbers provided by management.

Many small businesses understate income on their tax returns while their owners skim cash sales or claim creative deductions to avoid paying corporate taxes. Other sellers may overstate sales or distort their financials to create profits to facilitate a sale. The adverse tax consequences are considered a good investment when measured against the higher price these profits bring.

> *note* Inaccurate financials are not always accidental nor the result of poor accounting. Many small businesses don't show a profit, yet are highly profitable.

CAUTION

While accountants understand the reliability that attaches to the auditor's statements, buyers who review these same statements may not understand the significance of the auditor's opinions. Statements prepared by a CPA but labeled "unaudited" or "prepared from records without audit" are no more reliable because they are CPA prepared. They remain only the representations of management. The statements then become no more accurate than their sources.

DEFINITION

Audited statements vary in reliability depending on the nature of the accountant's opinion. There are four types of opinions:

1) *An unqualified opinion* means that the financial statements fairly present the business's financial position and the results of the operations.

2) *A qualified opinion* indicates that the financial statements in some material are not in conformity with generally accepted accounting principles applied on a consistent basis.

3) *An adverse opinion* is an opinion that the financial statements do not materially or fairly represent the financial position or results of operation in conformity with generally accepted accounting principles.

4) *A disclaimer of opinion* means that the auditor has not obtained sufficient information to form an opinion as to whether the financial statements as a whole result in a fair presentation.

In some situations that require a disclaimer of opinion on the overall fairness of the financial statements, the auditor may justify a partial opinion, certifying the accuracy of parts of the statement while offering either a qualified opinion or a disclaimer as to others.

The scope of financial analysis

The most intensive financial investigation is needed when the buyer is to purchase corporate shares because the financial representations concern the affairs of the corporation to be acquired. The financial investigation may be significantly relaxed under an asset transfer because hidden liabilities and other financial antecedents are not carried over to the buyer. In many cases the buyer's confidence in the seller's financial statements dictates whether it will be an asset or stock sale.

> *note* Only when the buyer believes the corporate books are "clean" is a stock sale considered.

When assets are to be acquired, the financial investigation will focus more on the income statements than the balance sheet. When the business will continue to be operated by the buyer without significant change, its future will be an extension of its past.

The buyer may be primarily buying the seller's location or customers' lists, technology or other assets which the buyer will reshape into a totally different business. The buyer may then have little interest in the seller's past performance, so the financial audit must have a focus as well as scope. For an intelligent audit, the buyer's accountant must understand the reason for the acquisition, the future business goals, how the business will change, and how those changes will influence profitability.

The three stages of financial investigation

The financial investigation generally evolves during the acquisition process through three distinct stages:

1) The preliminary stage

The preliminary stage focuses on whether the business qualifies as a potential acquisition, and the buyer determines whether or not the business has the sales, profits or growth potential to justify further pursuit.

The buyer frames his offer and visualizes how the deal may come together. In most cases, the parties agree in principle based only on the buyer's preliminary investigation. Few buyers undertake the cost of a more extensive investigation unless an acceptable deal can first be arranged. When the transaction requires further financial investigation, the agreement is made conditional upon an acceptable auditor's opinion or "due diligence." It is not unusual to see the original transaction significantly change, either in price or structure, after the next stage—preacquisition audit.

2) The preacquisition audit stage

While the preliminary investigation focuses on the suitability of the business, the preacquisition audit verifies that the business is as represented. The shift is away from the more base business considerations and toward the audit of books and records to make certain the buyer gets what he bargained for.

3) The closing stage

The closing stage verifies the closing entries to make certain there are no adverse changes in the business between the dates of agreement and closing, and to verify that the buyer is obtaining the assets agreed upon as well as handling adjustments.

Coordinating the financial investigation

The financial investigation requires close coordination between the buyer, the seller and their accountants. Many problems can arise and many potential acquisitions are aborted because of these difficulties.

The most common problem is the buyer's gaining access to the seller's financial information. Frequently, buyers demand access to the seller's books and records too soon in the acquisition process. The seller may view such a request as an unjustified intrusion if the buyer has neither convinced the seller he is qualified to buy the business, or will buy on terms that are agreeable to the seller.

 The buyer must convince the seller that he is qualified to make the acquisition and that he has sufficient interest to justify releasing the desired information.

Other sellers unjustifiably refuse financial information, even when the buyer has sincere interest. These sellers may refuse access until the buyer places an offer and deposit on the business.

The seller should be prepared to release the information as buyer interest and negotiations warrant. At the preliminary stage, the buyer is entitled to see several years' financial statements. Audit of the books and records and disclosure of sensitive items—such as vendors, credit rating, customers' lists, and so forth—should come only when the parties are closer to agreement. The agreement would then be conditional upon an auditor's verification.

The buyer, for instance, can sign a confidentiality and nondisclosure agreement to receive financial and other sensitive information. An accountant hired by the buyer helps demonstrate a legitimate interest in the business, because the buyer is now incurring costs. To preserve confidentiality, the seller will be more comfortable with the books in the hands of an accountant rather than the potential buyer.

Documents for financial review

The financial investigation will depend on many factors, and the information required will also vary, but should include:

- profit and loss statements (for three to five years)

- balance sheets—for the same time periods

- statements of change in financial position—for the same time periods

- federal and state tax returns—for corresponding periods.

- corporate pension plan and profit-sharing plan, if any

- aged lists of secured and general creditors

- lists of products, customers or markets and contribution of each to overall sales

- physical inventories

- copies of fringe benefits, documents such as medical, pension and other benefits

- cash flow statements

- insurance policies

- credit reports and ratings from Dun & Bradstreet, and commercial credit reporting services

- ◆ general ledgers, journals and other supporting accounting documents

- ◆ bank records for the prior two years

Analyzing the income statement

The income statement is most important because it projects future profitability. To establish operating trends, the buyer must review the profit and loss statements for the prior three years and an interim income statement for the current year. A shorter tie review will distort long-term trends. The interim current statement shows whether suddenly reduced sales or other recent adverse trends prompt the sale.

The income statement review should answer these questions:

1) Income

- • Are sales increasing or decreasing?

- • Are sales cyclical or steady?

- • Do sales depend upon one or more primary customers?

The buyer must understand the industry statistics. Therefore, industry statistics must be obtained.

- • How are sales divided between product lines? Markets? Customers?

- • What factors can adversely influence future sales?

- • What is the business true sales potential?

- • What change or cost is required to achieve this sales potential?

- • Do sales include extraordinary or non-recurring items?

- • Are sales reported on the cash or accrual method?

2) Gross Profits (Margins)

- Are gross profits above or below industry averages?

- What are the margins for each product line?

- Has pricing recently changed?

- Does the buyer purchase goods on unusually advantageous terms?

- Do certain customers or employees buy at a reduced price?

- Are margins based on an actual or estimated inventory appraisal?

- Have accounts payable been reconciled to reflect accurate margins?

- What percentage of sales is lost to shrinkage?

- What recent inventory markdowns or write-offs have adversely affected margins?

- Can sales/margins/profits be improved by price changes?

- What are the past and future margin trends for the industry? For the business?

3) Expenses

- Are total expenses (as a percentage of sales) above or below industry averages?

- Are individual expense items above or below industry averages?

- Are expenses reported on the cash or accrual method?

- How are expenses divided among production, administration and selling?

- What are the general and administrative expenses (if the business is a division or subsidiary of a larger company)?

- Is payroll too low? Too high?

- Is the owner's salary accurate?

- Will rent increase (as a percentage of sales) over the lease term?

4) Profitability

- What are the profit trends?

- What are the profits as a percentage of sales?

- How do profits compare to industry averages?

- What is the present return on investment?

- What is the buyer's projected return on investment?

- Are profits accurate?

- What are the true operational profits after extraordinary items?

Analyzing the balance sheet

The balance sheet gives the buyer valuable insights needed to negotiate the transaction and strategize tax and financing matters. Points to review:

1)   Assets (cash and receivables)

- Does the business have sufficient working capital?

- Has working capital changed significantly?

- Does the business have a positive or negative cash flow?

- What is the collection period on accounts receivables?

- Is credit too lenient or restrictive?

- What customers owe the most receivables?

- Does any one customer owe a significant receivable?

- What is the credit rating for larger customers?

- What credit guarantees or security is there for non-rated accounts?

- Are bad debts reasonable?

- What receivables are in collection, and what is their collectability?

- Are any receivables pledged or factored?

> **HOT spot** For asset transactions, the seller's balance sheet is less important to the buyer. For stock transfers, the balance sheet analysis becomes critical.

2) Inventories

- How is the inventory divided among finished goods, work-in-process and raw materials?

- How are inventories divided among departments, products or lines?

- What is the value of the inventory?

- What inventory is on consignment?

- What inventory is obsolete? Slow-moving?

- Is inventory excessive or depleted? Why?

- Is the inventory mix proper? (Plant, property and equipment)

- What is the acquisition price for the equipment?

- What is the equipment's fair market value?

- How is equipment depreciated?

- What remaining depreciation is available to the buyer?

- Is the equipment list complete?

- Are all capital assets free and clear of encumbrances?

- What capital assets can be sold?

3) Liabilities

- How is the debt divided between current and long term liabilities?

- What is the average aging on accounts payables?

- Are trade debts paid on time?

- Are any obligations in collection? In suit?

- Are any contingent or disputed liabilities not included on the financial statement?

- What is the company's credit rating?

- Are tax obligations current?

- Are debts due to officers or stockholders?

- What debts are secured? Unsecured?

- Are loans current and in good standing?

- Do any loans restrict operations?

- Can the company fully amortize its debts?

4) Capital

- What is the business' net worth or owner's equity?

- What are its retained earnings?

- Have dividends been declared in the past?

- Have there been recent contributions to capital?

- Are all shares fully paid and non-assessable?

- How is the capital stock distributed between the stockholders?

Tax return analysis

Compare federal and state tax returns to the financials. Review the current year's tax returns and returns for recent years not audited by the Internal Revenue Service. At stake are the potential tax liabilities. Deficiencies assessed against the company in earlier years should be reviewed to determine the adequacy of any tax reserves for subsequent unaudited years. Reviewing the tax returns also:

- Verifies operating loss carryovers and unused investment credits that may be beneficial to the buyer.

- Determines whether an accumulated earnings tax might be imposed on the selling corporation for the improper accumulation of surplus.

- Uncovers future tax savings possibilities not previously taken advantage of.

Interpreting the results

Ratio analysis used to evaluate managerial performance also helps evaluate the target business. The buyer is most interested in ratios that highlight operational weaknesses and strengths that will carry over to the buyer.

Ratios show relationships between the components of the financial statements. The acceptability of a ratio requires comparison with industry standards, which have their limitations because industry averages are only averages and cannot reflect unique characteristics of the business. Comparative analysis should then be an approximate guide rather than a rigid standard.

Ratio analysis should focus on the following:

Solvency ratios

The solvency ratio is important to the buyer only if the buyer plans a stock purchase. For the financially-weak company, the buyer must plan a turnaround. The buyer may invest more capital or otherwise reduce the debt (typically a Chapter 11 reorganization) or a combination of both.

Key solvency ratios include:

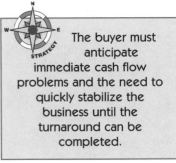

- current ratio (current assets divided by current liabilities)

- acid test ratio (cash, receivables and inventory divided by current liabilities)

The buyer must anticipate immediate cash flow problems and the need to quickly stabilize the business until the turnaround can be completed.

- debt to equity ratio (total debts divided by net worth)

Operating ratios

The operating ratios pinpoint managerial efficiency. The importance of the operating ratios to the buyer depends on the buyer's plans for the company. With an asset transfer and a completely redesigned operation, the business's historical inefficiencies are irrelevant to the buyer. Nevertheless, the profit evaluation depends on operating ratios as the buyer must estimate whether poor profits are due more to managerial deficiencies or external factors.

Numerous ratios measure operating efficiency:

- net sales to receivables (to determine charge sales versus cash sales)

- inventory turnover (to measure excess or slow-moving inventory)

- fixed asset turnover

- cost of sales per sales dollar

- returns to total sales (for quality control analysis)

- sales discounts to net sales

- purchase discounts to purchases

- indirect labor expense to direct labor expense

- maintenance expense to fixed expense (to determine the condition of equipment)

- net sales to current assets (to determine current asset turnover)

- net sales to working capital (for working capital turnover)

- net sales to plant investment (to determine plant utilization)

- net sales to total assets (to determine utilization of assets)

- net income to net worth (to measure return to stockholders on invested capital)

- operating expenses to sales using an itemized approach to determine excessive line items

Profitability ratios

The profit evaluation must be viewed from several perspectives. The buyer must measure how profits compare to similar businesses. With poor profits, the evaluation must identify the causes and possible cures, whether the poor profits are caused internally by inefficient management or from market, industry or competitive problems.

 A poorly performing business is acquired only if the buyer can make the business profitable.

Profit trends over several years can show improving or deteriorating profits. Fluctuating profits may be more easily explained in a cyclical industry, but rapid fluctuations in stable industries almost always signal operational or accounting change.

Two ratios measure profitability: "Profit to sales" and "profit to net worth" (return-on-investment). The second ratio is more meaningful from an investment viewpoint. However, management must always consider both. Many excellent companies operate with low profits as a percentage of sales but yield exceptionally high returns on investment.

Profit planning

With profit planning, there are two errors to avoid. The first extends profit trends to produce an aesthetically pleasant graph which seldom corresponds to reality. Future profits are controlled by many variables; this leads to the second common error: over-optimism in forecasting profits.

Many business failures result from this optimism. A buyer who optimistically foresees turning chronic losses into healthy profits may base his price and financing on these anticipated profits, only to end up with an overpriced business and loan defaults when the profits don't materialize. The objective is to reduce speculation and estimate profit conservatively.

The buyer must foresee operational changes and anticipated impact on sales, margins and expenses. The accountant must accurately reduce this to a pro-forma income statement and cash flow forecast. The accountant must also force the buyer to validate all assumptions on which projections are based.

The accountant must challenge not only the planned changes from a profit viewpoint, but the ability of the buyer to implement those changes. The accountant cannot blindly accept the buyer's predictions but must instead interject reality and objectivity to neutralize buyer optimism.

Analysis of the seller's financial statements is meaningless unless the buyer can translate past profitability into reasonably accurate profit projections.

With seller financing, the profit planning equally concerns the seller. The ability of the business to pay the seller's note depends on future profits, a commonly overlooked point. Many sellers, anxious to sell for an inflated price, extend substantial financing that soon defaults unless the buyer can pay the note from sources other than profits. The seller must always question how his note will be paid from the business.

There is no one right approach to profit planning. The procedure is far less important than caution. The buyer must thoroughly analyze each item on the seller's financials to prevent overestimating income or underestimating expenses, so the buyer can determine:

- the desirability of the acquisition

- the price to pay

- the financing the business can handle

- problems that may remain after the acquisition

- opportunities to improve the business

The legal investigation

Chapter 5
The legal investigation

What you'll find in this chapter:

⟹ The legal investigation checklist

⟹ The corporate/organizational review

⟹ Property and contracts reviews

⟹ The liabilities review

⟹ The litigation and claims review

note

The legal investigation should begin after the financial investigation is completed and the preliminary decision is made to buy the business. A comprehensive legal analysis is usually unjustified earlier, since prospective acquisitions are frequently rejected after the financial analysis.

The legal investigation is usually staggered along with the business and financial investigation. For example, leases and liabilities may be preliminarily reviewed before negotiations and structuring the deal. Other legal items may be reviewed upon drafting the contract, and others are preclosing matters. Important items should be checked before contract signing.

The attorney's opinion letter

If the seller's counsel provides certain warranties and representations about the company, the seller's counsel may request an opinion letter from the buyer's counsel concerning the buyer. In certain instances, counsel will issue a qualified or "without recourse" opinion, which increases the need for independent verification.

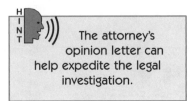

The attorney's opinion letter can help expedite the legal investigation.

The counsel's opinion essentially guarantees his warranties and representations. Should they prove untrue, he can have liability. That is why opinions are narrowly confined only to items personally verified by the lawyer.

The legal investigation checklist

What the buyer's counsel must review will depend on many factors, including:

- the nature of the business

- the transactional structure (assets or shares)

- the investment and risk factor

- the extent to which the buyer is familiar or presently involved with the business

Many items in the legal investigation also may be reviewed by the accountant in the financial analysis. Some overlap is beneficial. The buyer's counsel must review items in six categories:

1) The corporate/organizational review

The corporate or organizational review chiefly depends on whether the buyer will acquire shares or assets. Where the buyer acquires the seller's corporation, the buyer must thoroughly verify corporate affairs. For asset transfers the investigation can focus on the corporate existence and the authority to transfer good title. A more comprehensive investigation would:

- Verify the date and state of incorporation, including all subsidiaries.

- Verify that all annual filings are current and that the corporation is in good standing.

- Verify authorized capital stock by classes, indicating the number of shares and their par value, as well as the rights and privileges of holders of each class of stock.

- Review the corporate purpose to ascertain whether contemplated corporate activities are authorized.

- Review the articles of incorporation, by-laws and amendments.

- Obtain a complete stockholder's list and verify possible conversion of preferred stocks or bonds to common stocks.

- Verify that there are no outstanding stock subscriptions, options, warrants or preemptive rights.

- Verify whether there are outstanding proxies, powers of attorney, voting trusts or other assignments of right to any shares.

- Verify that all shares are free and clear of pledge or other encumbrance and are fully paid for and non-assessable.

- Obtain a list of states in which the corporation and each subsidiary is authorized to do business, the qualification date, the name and address of their statutory agent, and whether the corporation (or subsidiary) remains qualified to do business as a foreign corporation.

- For a partnership, obtain the partnership agreement and all amendments.

- Investigate the filing of assumed name certificates.

2) Property review

- Obtain a description of all real estate to be included as part of the transaction.

- For real estate to be acquired, obtain copies of all mortgages, liens or other encumbrances, including leases against the property.

- For land or buildings to be acquired, obtain the date of acquisition, age of the building, construction type, depreciation rates used and the accumulated depreciation. Verify all titles, policies, title opinions, appraisals, surveys, and all agreements relating to or affecting the real property, including zoning, building, or health code reports.

If the property is leased, obtain copies of all leases, amendments to leases, assignments or sublets in effect, and obtain an estoppel letter from the lessor acknowledging the current status of the lease.

- Obtain a description and age of the principle items or classes of machinery or equipment to be acquired, and a schedule showing their total cost, depreciation reserve, depreciation rates used and allowed by the Internal Revenue Service, including investment credits allowed or anticipated.

- Obtain a listing of encumbrances, security agreements, conditional sales agreements or financing agreements on any items of machinery, equipment or other capital assets to be acquired, including copies of all agreements and verification of the balances owed.

- Obtain a list of all capital assets, including office furniture, equipment or machinery to which the seller does not have title, including all items on loan, bailment, lease or personally owned by officers or employees.

- Obtain a list of all inventory, raw material, goods in process or available for resale to which the seller does not have clear title. This should include goods held on consignment, sale on approval, bailment or otherwise segregated for sale and shipment under an existing purchase agreement.

3) The intangible property review

- Review all accounts receivable, including names of each account debtor, address, amount due and account status. Verify whether any account has filed a claim, reason for nonpayment or if any other notice has been received, impairing the ability to collect—such as a notice of bankruptcy.

- Verify the accounts receivable in collection. This should include the name of an attorney or collection agency, fee arrangements and a written report on the probability for collection.

- For factored receivables, obtain copies of factoring agreements and accounts covered by the factoring arrangement. Determine whether the factor has rights of recourse and whether there are any pending or prospective claims on recourse.

- Verify notes receivable due the corporation, also including amounts due, compliance with payment schedules, security agreements, and reserves for anticipated uncollectibles.

- Review all negotiable and non-negotiable securities held and to be acquired under the transaction. Verify their acquisition date, cost basis, present market value and any possible restrictions on transfer.

- Review all trademarks, patents and copyrights owned or used in the business, and for each their registration number, date of registration, registrant and use.

- Review employee confidentiality agreements, nondisclosures and employee participation programs involving the development and safeguard of intangible proprietary rights.

- Verify pension, ERISA or employee benefit plans to be included or acquired under the transaction, including the balance amount, compliance with funding and tax requirements, trustees and depositories of funds, amounts borrowed and assignability requirements.

4) The contracts review

On an acquisition of corporate shares, buyer's counsel must review all binding agreements. On a sale of assets the same requirements exist for contracts or obligations to be assumed and counsel must also verify the contracts are assignable. The seller's counsel will want to terminate the seller's liability upon assumption of the contracts by the buyer.

The first step is to define the executory contracts to be assumed by the buyer and the cancellation rights with other contracts. The buyer's counsel also must:

- Review employment contracts, bonus arrangements, profit sharing or similar compensation/benefit programs for executives or employees.

- Review union contracts and the strikes, organizing activity or collective bargaining issues that may arise.

- Review supplier and vendor agreements that obligate the company to future purchases, and verify their terms and conditions.

- Review purchase orders and sales contracts accepted by the company.

- Review insurance policies, amount of coverage, exclusions, deductibles and loss payees.

- Review service contracts including contracts for maintenance of properties, equipment (including warranty agreements), and contracts on such items as burglar alarms, rubbish disposal, and telephone equipment.

- Review service contracts or warranties issued to customers by the company.

- Review brokerage agreements relative to the proposed sale, including co-brokerage agreements.

- Review retainer agreements with attorneys, accountants, consultants, public relations firms, advertising agencies and other professionals.

- Review advertising and promotional contracts including media contracts, billboard rentals and other space advertising.

- Review contracts and purchase orders for all goods on order or items made to specification.

5) The liabilities review

A review of liabilities—actual or contingent—is necessary to ascertain liabilities knowingly assumed and to assess the likelihood of creditor claims and transferee liability against the buyer.

For the seller, the liability issue concerns discharging liabilities from the sales proceeds (under an asset transfer) or protecting the seller (or principals under any guarantees) from those liabilities to be assumed by the buyer or that remain unpaid upon the sale.

The liability analysis includes:

1) Review all secured debts for:

- creditor identification

- collateral

- obligation terms

- interest

- amortization

- maturity

The buyer must also check the conditions of assignability on any secured debt if an encumbered asset is to be transferred. Verification should include all secured debts under the Uniform Commercial Code, including conditional sales agreements and lease/purchase agreements and recordings of financing statements and the proper perfection of the secured transaction.

2) Review all tax liabilities including:

- tax liabilities due the Internal Revenue Service, including FICA, unemployment compensation

- taxes due the state or municipalities for withholding tax, excise, sales or use tax, meals tax, personal property tax or similar tariffs

3) Verify loans to the corporation from insiders, including:

- officers and stockholders

- the balance owed—whether the loan is subordinated to other debts

4) Verify all other priority obligations and the identification of each creditor, amount due and terms.

5) Review all accounts payable and trade indebtedness, including:

- creditor's name and address

- amount due

- adjustments for credits and interest

- whether disputed or undisputed

6) Review all accrued but unpaid expenses including:

- payroll (and vacation pay and fringe benefits)

- rents

- utilities

- insurance

- advertising

7) Identify each obligation secured by personal guarantees or whether any other party is primarily or secondarily liable on the debt.

8) Verify company borrowing from pension or profit sharing plans.

9) Verify obligations due to any affiliated company.

6) The litigation and claims review

Examining liabilities extends to those that are known, undisputed and unliquidated. More important are unknown, disputed or contingent claims. Litigation may involve both claims asserted by and against the company.

For pending litigation—regardless whether the company is plaintiff or defendant—a full statement of the issues, the nature of the litigation, the amount in dispute, the probable settlement value and probable outcome, are matters that can be provided by the seller's counsel. Nevertheless, even if subject to seller indemnification, the buyer's counsel should carefully review the merits and potential impact on the company.

> *note*
> While pending or threatened litigation may be protected against, it's difficult to accurately speculate on future problems or claims that may arise from the sale itself.

Litigation claims may be adequately covered by insurance. Buyer's counsel must evaluate potential recovery against insurance coverage to estimate a possible deficiency for which the company will be liable.

Investigative procedures

Disclosure will necessarily be forthright. Active seller concealment extends to legal as well as financial matters. Or the seller may simply overlook or underestimate matters of legal importance.

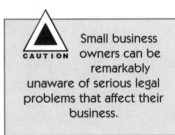

CAUTION Small business owners can be remarkably unaware of serious legal problems that affect their business.

If the buyer has adequate indemnification for undisclosed liabilities, the importance of the legal investigation obviously lessens. Even then, problems can be more than a nuisance for a buyer who must resolve the matter before seeking indemnification from the seller.

How to structure the sale

Chapter 6

How to structure the sale

What you'll find in this chapter:

- ➠ Different ways to acquire a business
- ➠ Factors to consider
- ➠ Fees and taxes
- ➠ Methods of transfer
- ➠ Tax-free reorganizations

There are several ways to acquire a business, and choosing the best method involves complex business, financial, legal and tax considerations for both the buyer and seller. The accountants and attorneys for the buyer and seller must assist in deciding upon the method of transfer.

The methods of sale

Sale of assets

The seller sells the business' assets to the buyer for cash, notes or equity securities in the buyer's corporation. After selling the business assets to the buyer, the selling corporation may continue to function as a private holding or investment company for its shareholders, and thus create a taxable gain or loss to the corporation. More commonly, the selling corporation liquidates and passes any taxable gain or loss on to its shareholders.

If the seller operates a sole proprietorship or partnership, the sale must be through the sale and transfer of assets, since there are no corporate shares for the buyer to acquire. This is a particularly important point because so many small businesses are unincorporated. While it is difficult to estimate the percentage of small businesses transferred through a sale of assets, its simplicity makes it the most common method.

Sale of corporate shares

The existing shareholders sell their corporate shares to the buyer. Upon acquisition of the corporate shares, the buyer usually obtains the resignation of the present officers and directors and installs its own management, gaining both ownership and managerial control.

As with an asset sale, the buyer may pay cash, notes or securities. However, in this instance, the consideration is paid directly to the selling stockholders, usually creating for them a taxable gain or deductible loss.

Redemption sale

DEFINITION

A *redemption sale* is similar to the sale of corporate shares and is an indirect approach to the same result. The selling stockholders sell or redeem their shares back to the corporation which then retires the purchased shares as non-voting treasury stock. The corporation, as buyer, directly pays the stockholders with cash, notes or a transfer of other corporate assets. Simultaneous with the redemption by the selling shareholders, the buyer subscribes to new shares, and becomes the new stockholder of the corporation.

As with a direct sale of corporate shares, the buyer as the new stockholder appoints new officers and directors, to gain ownership and managerial control over the corporation.

A redemption is primarily used when the selling stockholders intend to finance part of the purchase price and requires as collateral a security interest on the corporate assets. By selling the shares to the corporation instead of to the buyer, the obligation to pay becomes primarily that of the corporation, thus justifying the corporation granting a security interest to secure its own indebtedness. This corporation obligation is normally guaranteed by the buyer.

Statutory merger

DEFINITION

Mergers are similar to asset sales. However, with *statutory mergers* the seller receives shares of the buyer's corporation instead of cash or notes. While this closely compares to asset sales, the mechanics and tax rules are quite different. In the Model Business Corporation Act, the corporation to be acquired does not terminate its business, but becomes a subsidiary of the acquiring corporation.

> *note*
> Within the context of small business transfers, statutory mergers usually involve affiliated companies desiring tax-free reorganizations.

Consolidation

DEFINITION

Consolidation means that two or more existing corporations combine and create a new successor corporation. It is not usually necessary to file new articles of organization to create a new corporation if the statutory requirements are followed. As with statutory mergers, consolidations are uncommon in small business transfers. When two small business owners desire to pool their business interests to form a jointly owned larger enterprise, they generally prefer the statutory merger or tax-free reorganization.

Factors to consider when structuring the sale

No one factor usually controls how the sale is structured, because there are competing advantages and disadvantages. But one factor may outweigh all other factors and dictate how the deal comes together.

Fifteen factors influence the type transfer:

1) Liability protection

A buyer wants to be protected against unknown or contingent liabilities of the seller. A purchase of assets best insulates the buyer from the seller's liabilities, provided the assets are clear of liens and encumbrances, and the buyer complies with the Bulk Sales Act. If the sale is for fair consideration and is not a fraudulent transfer, the buyer should have no further concern for the seller's liabilities. This broad buyer protection argues strongly for an asset sale, and buyers commonly insist on an asset sale for this one reason alone.

> To determine the potential risk from undisclosed or contingent liabilities, the buyer must consider not only his recourse, but the likelihood of a creditor claim.

The buyer's worry over undisclosed liabilities is far greater under a stock sale since undisclosed or contingent creditors can continue to assert their claim against the acquired corporation. The buyer's concern, even under a stock transfer, will depend on the buyer's protection under the stock sale through strong indemnification.

2) Leases

In a sale of assets, the buyer entity must obtain a new lease, unless the selling corporation can assign its lease. This is uncommon. By purchasing the seller's shares the corporation and its lease remain undisturbed.

If the seller has a long, low-rent lease it is advantageous for the buyer to acquire the corporation. The alternative is to buy assets and face a higher rent on a new lease. If rents are rapidly escalating, the savings to the buyer can be significant.

HINT The buyer may need to negotiate a new lease in either circumstance if the existing lease will soon expire.

3) Financing

Financing can determine if it will be a sale of assets or shares. If the corporation has high debts, the buyer can easily use these debts as a credit toward the purchase price under a stock sale. Although debts also can be assumed by a buyer in an asset transfer, it's easier to accomplish through a stock sale. If the corporation's assets are secured and these debts are to be assumed by the buyer as part of the purchase price, it is necessary to obtain creditor approval. Utilizing debts to help finance an acquisition is common in takeovers of financially distressed companies where the buyer acquires the corporate shares at a nominal price and then restructures the corporate debt.

note A seller cannot convey encumbered assets without creditor approval. Creditor approval is not required in a stock sale.

4) Contracts

The corporation may hold non-assignable contract rights such as franchises, distributorship agreements or supplier contracts. Acquiring the corporate shares leaves these corporate contracts intact. An asset transfer requires their assignment and approval.

Important contracts usually argue for a stock sale. However, under a transfer of assets, the business may shed undesirable or burdensome contracts. A seller's breach of its agreements under an asset transfer should concern the buyer as the other party to the contract would then become a creditor of the selling corporation for his damages. The buyer under an asset transfer must then require the same indemnification as with other liabilities.

5) Labor unions

Labor unions and collective bargaining agreements can be serious obstacles to asset transfers. There is no requirement for mandatory collective bargaining in a corporate change, but it is more likely the union will demand a new contract in a sale of assets. Clearly the buyer of assets is bound to accept the collective bargaining contracts of the selling corporation where the business is sold as an ongoing enterprise.

HOT spot There is increased possibility of a more burdensome union agreement under an asset sale—particularly if the buyer is financially stronger than the seller.

6) Employee benefit plans

Are the selling corporation's employee benefit plans compatible with the buyer's? This may influence the transaction. If the seller's plans are substantially more expensive than the buyer's, it may be worthwhile for the buyer to operate the acquisition as a subsidiary.

In an asset transfer, the buyer will usually be required to terminate the old plan and pay out the vested amount or freeze the old plan and hold the amount accumulated in trust for the employees until they terminate their employment. Whether the seller's existing benefit plans are an asset or liability to the buyer depends upon their level of funding and the actuarial assumptions on which they are based. This requires review by a pension specialist.

7) Credit rating

The corporation's credit rating can either be an advantage or disadvantage. A good credit rating favors the purchase of shares so the buyer obtains the continued benefit of the corporation's rating. A buyer's newly created corporation must start with no credit.

Conversely, a buyer may do better with a new corporation, and limited or no credit, rather than take over a corporation with a poor rating. This can be important, particularly for the buyer who needs credit to augment for limited working capital.

8) Corporate charters

A stock transaction preserves the corporate charter when this is important. For example, the corporation may hold a banking or insurance charter which may be difficult for the buyer to obtain. Here a convincing case can be made for a stock sale.

When the selling corporation operates in several states, it may be easier to acquire shares rather than undergo the laborious process of qualifying a new corporation in each of these jurisdictions. This is also true when the corporation holds numerous or difficult-to-obtain licenses or permits.

9) Partial sales

If the parties contemplate a sale of only part of the business, the seller usually wants to sell specific assets and have the corporation continue in operation with the remaining assets. But this does not always preclude the sale of the corporation. The retained assets can alternatively be transferred to the stockholders of the selling corporation as a distribution upon liquidation while the buyer acquires the corporation.

The primary consideration in a partial sale is the amount of assets to be sold versus those to be retained by the seller and whether the seller will continue the business.

10) Stockholder approvals

If the selling corporation is owned by a number of stockholders, the sale of stock requires agreement from all stockholders—assuming the buyer wants 100 percent ownership—which is generally the case with small businesses. If minority stockholders refuse to sell their shares, then selling the corporate assets becomes the only alternative. The seller and buyer then share the responsibility to see that the corporate authority to sell, and the sale itself, is proper to avoid litigation from dissenting minority stockholders. The parties also must see that a proper stockholders' meeting was held to vote on the proposed sale in conformity with the by-laws.

The critical issue is whether the business is being sold for a plausible business purpose and at a fair price. Anticipating a minority stockholder objection, the parties should solicit approval of the sale from stockholders early in the negotiation and commit the assenting stockholders to prevent a later change in position.

11) Tax considerations

While small business transfers seldom involve the complex tax problems of the large corporate merger or consolidation, tax strategies can nevertheless influence choice of structure. The two predominant tax considerations are:

- the possibility of an increased basis for depreciable assets in an asset sale

- the possibility of a tax-loss carryforward under a sale of corporate shares

The potential for an increased basis is useful for later depreciation. It exists when capital assets are carried on the seller's books at a low book value and the buyer can allocate a substantial part of the price to these assets and establish a new basis for later depreciation.

Acquiring corporate shares essentially deprives the buyer of the tax savings on future profits that would otherwise be shielded through the depreciation available on a higher basis. This may or may not pose a reciprocal disadvantage for the seller. If the seller plans to liquidate his corporation, the corporation would escape the capital-gains tax resulting from the difference between the selling price and book value. Here the stockholders pay a capital gains tax on the entire distribution less the cost basis for their shares regardless of how the price is allocated among the various assets.

> *note* With a tax-loss, the buyer's accountant must validate the loss to ensure the buyer can defend the tax-loss carryforward in the event of a later tax audit.

A tax-loss carryforward can be a compelling reason to purchase shares. The economic benefit of the tax-loss carryforward must be profiled against probable future profits within the carryforward period.

12) Transfer taxes

There may be state and local taxes on a transfer of assets. Franchise and property taxes are examples. Because some states charge as much as a 10 percent sales tax on personal property transferred under an asset sale, the tax can be significant. It is frequently possible to reduce the tax by apportioning much of the price to goodwill, with the disadvantage that the buyer loses depreciation on tangible assets.

13) Corporate name

The corporate name may be an important asset and may be obtainable only through purchase of the corporation under a stock sale. However, the name can be sold to the buyer under an asset sale for use without the corporate designation. The buyer would then incorporate under its own corporate name and adopt the buyer's name as a trade style.

14) Insurance ratings

The corporation's experience rating with workman's compensation and unemployment may be valuable if it is significantly below the rating the buyer would receive as a new corporate entity.

15) Professional fees

Accounting and legal fees are usually less in an asset transfer than under a stock sale because it is simpler than a stock sale. A stock sale usually requires an intensive legal and financial investigation and a tightly drafted contract to protect and safeguard the buyer. A stock sale thus requires considerably more professional attention than an asset sale. There are exceptional cases where an asset sale may be more complex and time consuming than a stock sale, as when the business has many parcels of real estate to be conveyed or new licenses to be obtained.

Selecting the method of transfer

The buyer prefers one method of transfer and the seller another. Many transactions fail because the parties cannot agree on how to structure the deal, despite agreement on other items.

Most buyers prefer an asset sale. Sellers generally prefer a stock sale. The reason for these preferences is ordinarily one of priorities. Buyers are

> *note*
> Deciding the
> method of transfer
> is seldom decided upon
> legal considerations alone.

conscious of the potential liability problems that can result from a stock sale and prefer the cleaner asset transfer, some even when other advantages exist from takeover of the seller's corporation. Some attorneys refuse anything but an asset transfer, concerned about their ability to effectively protect their clients from undisclosed liabilities.

The parties must appreciate the various benefits under each method of transfer and blend the financial and business considerations into a decision that balances both risk and benefit. Selecting the method of transfer is neither the seller's nor the buyer's option. Both must weigh the advantages and disadvantages of each method of transfer from his own position, but be equally sensitive to the benefit and detriments to the other party.

Tax-free reorganizations

Tax-free reorganizations, mergers and consolidations reflect how so many large corporations are sold while tax-free reorganizations are generally inapplicable to privately owned small-business transactions. So this chapter only highlights their provisions. However, when such a transaction is planned, refer to the Internal Revenue Code and the vast body of case law supporting their interpretation and application.

There are, generally speaking, six types of reorganizations, classified respectively as A, B, C, D, E and F reorganizations. The A, B and C reorganizations deal primarily with corporate acquisitions. The D reorganization involves firms spinning off assets. The E reorganization covers recapitalization and F covers changes in corporate identity.

- **Type A Reorganization.** The Type A reorganization may be with a statutory merger or consolidation.

- **Type B Reorganization.** The acquisition by one corporation in exchange solely for all or part of its voting stock—or stock of another corporation. Immediately thereafter, the acquiring corporation gains control over the acquired corporation.

- **Type C Reorganization.** The acquisition by one corporation in exchange solely for all or part of its voting stock or substantially all of the properties of another corporation.

- **Type D Reorganization.** A transfer by a corporation of all or part of its assets to another corporation, if immediately after the transfer, the transferor or one or more of its stockholders in control of the transferee corporation and the transferee corporation distributes securities pursuant to Section 354, 355, or 356 of the Internal Revenue Code.

- **Type E Reorganization.** Bondholders or stockholders exchange their holdings for other forms of debt or equity for purposes of rearranging the financial structure of the corporation with no increase in earnings, profits or assets.

- **Type F Reorganization.** The corporation merely changes its name, state of incorporation or form of business existence otherwise retaining the same ownership.

How to value the business

7

Chapter 7

How to value the business

Both the buyer and seller must ask: How can the business be best valued? What methods can be used to value the company? How do they differ? When should each be used? Is the business being sold or acquired at too high or too low a price?

Small business valuation is far from a precise science. No one equation deals effectively with all the factors that must be considered. Valuation essentially blends many subjective and objective considerations, and reduces it to a perceived value which must be closely shared between buyer and seller if a sale is to be consummated.

Three valuation trouble spots

The worth of a large company can be easily determined from the trading value of its stock. This is not true of the small business whose valuation is made more difficult because of several unique valuation problems:

1) Lack of accurate records

Many small businesses lack records to show the true performance of the enterprise. The seller may be the only individual who knows the value of the business as an income producer and values the business on those earnings, including hidden benefits realized from the business. If the seller is unable to prove these profits, the buyer may set a far lower valuation.

2) The human element

Small businesses are extensions of the seller, who develops an emotional as well as a financial relationship with the business, particularly when the seller owned the business for many years. The seller who has started the business and nurtured it to maturity won't objectively value the business using strict economic yardsticks. This is why many small businesses are overpriced and remain unsold.

HOT spot Human emotion cannot change the value of the business, but emotion is an obstacle if it prevents the seller from selling at a reasonable price.

3) Future changes

The buyer's value of the business must be based on what the business can earn for him, not the seller. However, forecasting future profits is difficult. Small businesses are volatile income producers. The business may center on one or two people and its success mirrors their contribution, which success may or may not be duplicated by the buyer.

Small businesses may double or triple their sales and earnings under new management. But many other businesses shrink. To the extent the buyer buys an economic future, that financial future may be too different from its present to easily evaluate.

Common appraisal methods to avoid

Small businesses are too often valued by overly simplistic "rule of thumb" formulas. These conventional yardsticks are convenient to use, yet they fail because they do not value the business based on its future profitability. They instead rely on less relevant measures. Here are four appraisal formulas to avoid:

1) **The Sales Multiplier Method.** Every industry has a rough formula to translate sales into an approximate value. Supermarkets, for example, are priced at inventory plus one month's sales. Luncheonettes and small restaurants are commonly valued at three to four months sales. Drugstores are supposed to sell for about 100 days' sales.

> **⚠ CAUTION** Sales can be an important valuation factor if the buyer can somehow project proportionate profits. But lacking that profit projection, the sales multiplier remains a faulty valuation technique.

Sales multipliers cannot accurately value a business because a multiplier only considers sales and disregards profits. The sales multiplier makes sense only if the profits of a business coincide with its sales, which is rarely the case; the sales of a small business and the profit seldom correlate. A business with substantial sales may have equally substantial losses. A small volume enterprise may, in turn, be a big profit producer.

2) **The Comparison Method.** Valuations, to some buyers and sellers, are nothing more than comparing the target business' price against the price asked for comparable businesses. This is not necessarily a poor approach. The value of anything is largely based on prices

charged for comparable items. Because market conditions influence value, both the buyer and seller should negotiate with a clear idea of what competitive businesses sell for.

The difficulty with comparing businesses is that unlike most other items, businesses cannot be accurately compared. Since earnings depend on the individual characteristics of the business (i.e. volume, expenses, loan terms, competition and potential), businesses seldom have sufficient points of

Businesses are complex economic entities with many variables.

similarity to allow credible comparisons. When comparisons are made, the focus is usually on sales so the approach becomes similar to the sales multiplier. This may not be as true with buyers who thoroughly investigated the financial affairs of other ventures, but it is for sellers who only know a competitor's sales and selling price.

Franchised businesses are an exception. Franchising is based on conformity, and franchised operations with comparable sales should show comparable profits or profit margins, expenses and other operating costs that closely conform to chain standards.

3) *The Asking Price Method.* Another common but faulty approach is to believe that value somehow relates to the seller's "asking price." It may to the seller, but not to the buyer.

Many buyers use the asking price as a threshold to bargain. They believe that if they can negotiate the asking price down 15 or 25 percent, they have suddenly found "value." Buyers cannot assume that what the seller asks for the business bears any relationship to its value. A seller is the least qualified to determine the value of the business to a buyer. Buoyed by years of psychological attachment to the business and the obvious self-serving benefit of a high price, sellers frequently overprice their business. When the business sits unsold for a year or two, the seller gradually drops the price.

4) ***The Asset-Valuation Method.*** The most common method for valuing the small business is to value each asset to be sold, particularly when a business is primarily selling tangible assets.

For example, a seller may value the business at $100,000, and allocate $50,000 for inventory at wholesale cost, $25,000 as replacement or fair market value of the fixtures and equipment and $25,000 for goodwill. Of course, if other assets are to be sold, they would be similarly valued and added to the price.

> Rather than start at the top with the seller's asking price, the buyer should assume the business has no value and qualify every dollar he offers against the profit potential of the business.

Valuing a business by the sum of its assets has its own limitations. Tangible assets can be accurately appraised. Inventory can be precisely tabulated at its cost price. The approximate replacement value for fixtures and equipment can be obtained through outside appraisals. But goodwill has illusive value—and goodwill has other intangibles which must be included in most small business valuations.

Frequently, the value of goodwill and other intangibles exceeds the value of all tangible assets. The value of the business then is largely its goodwill. Since goodwill is only the anticipation of future profits, the buyer must still value those future profits.

> **note** Without a profit potential, tangible assets are worth only what they would bring at liquidation.

The business selling for the value of its tangible assets alone presents no easier a situation. A seller, for example, may offer to sell a retail business for the cost of its inventory and the replacement value of fixtures. But, what are those assets really worth if they cannot produce future profits?

Many marginal businesses are sold for the replacement value of their tangible assets, and each buyer assumes they have little at risk. But they are wrong. The buyer should buy a business only if it can become a profit producer.

The capitalized earnings valuation

The value of a business should be based on capitalized future earnings. Yet in most buy-sell transactions, the price is based on the asset value, not its profits. Profits are earned from assets. Assets are only incidental to those future profits.

The usual goal in business is to make money. Earnings, then, must dictate the value and the buyer must accurately measure those earnings and determine what those profits are worth to the buyer. Because proper valuation is most important when buying a business, the earnings forecast becomes critical. Good profit forecasting requires objectivity and careful projections to prepare a realistic pro-forma income statement.

When forecasting future profits, the buyer must consider historical profits. However, the seller's income statement won't project those future profits because the seller's profitability may differ from the buyer's. The seller's statements may also be inaccurate, conceal existing profits or even artificially inflate profits to induce a higher price. Historical analysis can nevertheless define certain ongoing costs and expenses.

Objectivity in forecasting is critical and the lack of a realistic forecast causes many buyers to buy at too high a price and fail. Inexperienced, optimistic buyers with a dangerous enthusiasm are all too common. Tempered optimism is desirable; unrealistic expectations are fatal. The buyer who forsees doubling sales from $200,000 to $400,000 within two years must ask himself if the $400,000 sales projection is realistic.

The income statement forecast should adopt a "worst case/best case" scenario, with an intermediate model for actual expectations. This three-pronged projection covers the widest range of eventualities.

CAUTION Lack of objectivity can distort the earnings forecast in many different ways. The buyer may similarly anticipate improved operating margins or reduced expenses.

Aside from projecting profits, forecasting forces the buyer to think through each phase of the business as he or she would operate it, and presented as clearly as in a business plan. To accomplish this the buyer must carefully project:

- *Sales.* What is the best estimate of existing sales? Are sales increasing or decreasing? What new sales will be generated? How? When? What are the assumptions for those future sales? What is required to produce those sales?

- *Cost of goods.* The buyer's profit margins (both as a percent of sales and in dollars) will differ from the seller's. New products may be added or deleted—or there may be changes to the merchandise mix, price or buying. How will these changes influence margins?

- *Owner's draw.* Disregard the seller's salary. An owner's salary should represent the fair value for the owner's managerial effort. An inflated salary diminishes profits, and a reduced salary inflates profits.

- *Payroll.* After sales, payroll is the second most difficult item to project. The seller's statement may have a payroll padded with family members who work for below-market wages.

- *Rent.* The seller's rent may be far lower than the buyer's as a new lease will probably be required, typically at a higher rent. A buyer cannot accurately forecast occupancy costs until the new rent is known.

- *Utilities.* Present utility costs can be easily verified but new equipment or renovations can materially increase these costs. Energy-intensive businesses should obtain cost estimates from electricians.

- *Depreciation.* The buyer's accountant normally attempts to allocate as much of the purchase price as possible to capital assets to maximize depreciation and reduce taxes.

- *Interest.* The seller may have little or no long-term debt and therefore pay little or no interest. The buyer usually requires financing and must estimate his financing and interest costs.

- *Advertising.* The buyer may need to increase advertising to increase sales. On the other hand, a seller contemplating a sale may wind down advertising.

- *Insurance.* Additional inventory, new fixtures, and lender requirements may require added insurance coverage. A cost estimate should be obtained from an insurance broker.

The earnings/valuation formula

With earnings projected, the buyer can convert those earnings into a value after considering several points.

First, the buyer must determine his or her minimally acceptable return on investment (ROI). For calculation purposes, if the buyer demands a 20 percent ROI and the business has a forecasted average annual earnings of $30,000, the business is worth about $150,000 ($30,000 x .20) to the buyer.

What should a buyer realistically expect as a return on investment? Since small businesses are unsafe investments, a 20 to 30 percent return is not excessive. But, the buyer must understand his or her investment objectives. Someone who buys for speculation with the objective of building the business for quick resale at a sizable profit, will expect a far higher return than one who buys only for operational profits.

 note Many turnaround speculators expect to double their investment in under two years.

Buyers may give little or no thought to their return on investment because buyers often buy with their heart—not their head. This is understandable. Buyers buy businesses to satisfy personal goals as well as financial goals.

HOT spot For the passive investor, ROI is the only objective. If the return is of secondary importance to the active manager, a well-documented forecast of healthy earnings is the only way to attract investment capital. Banks and other lenders also want assurance the business has the profit prospects to pay the loan.

If the buyer seeks a 20 percent ROI on a $150,000 investment, would the buyer expect to pay the same $150,000 for a business with $100,000 in tangible assets, compared to a service business with no tangible assets? Obviously asset values must be factored, but not to the point where the ROI becomes unacceptable.

Leverage is another consideration, and even points out the problem in defining the "investment" against which earnings must be measured. The buyer may logically look only to the down payment as his investment, and measure the available profits after subtracting interest on the financing. Other buyers use the total price, not cash down, as their yardstick.

Six factors that control price

DEFINITION

The ROI controls what the business is worth, but many other factors greatly influence what the business will sell for. *Value* is what the business is worth. But, value is not synonymous with price. *Price* is what the seller wants for the business, or will sell it for. If value is a function of appraised worth, price is a function of negotiation. The only relationship between the two is that value is the reference point from which price is negotiated. Nevertheless, value and price are mutually dependent. What affects one will affect the other. These influencing factors may adjust the valuation or negotiated price.

1) **Supply and demand.** The price of a business is influenced by the number of buyers compared to the number of businesses for sale. A "buyer's market" versus a "seller's market" may alter price by 20 percent or more. Rapid and huge price increases occur during times of high unemployment when the unemployed turn to small business ownership.

2) **Nature of the business.** Similar to supply and demand, the type of business also influences price. Many industries are on the decline and have

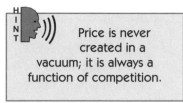

Price is never created in a vacuum; it is always a function of competition.

fewer interested buyers—and lower prices. Fading industries include independent clothing stores, hardware stores and drugstores. Independent convenience stores have regained popularity and now sell at a premium. Businesses that do not require specialized training and allow easy entry have historically sold for more than those with a more limited buyer market.

3) **Risk.** For many sellers, a reduced financial risk or "downside" justifies a higher price. And it is more than a reasonable concession. The buyer with little to lose—either in down payment or residual

liability—can afford a more generous price. Consider, for example, a buyer who acquires the shares of a corporation for only $15,000 down, using existing debts to finance the balance of a $150,000 price. This same buyer won't resist the $150,000 price as much as one who risks a $150,000 down payment or personal guarantees for that amount.

4) **Down payment.** A low down payment and the opportunity for a leveraged acquisition can influence price. Buyers focus more on down payment than on price. Price resistance decreases as the needed down payment decreases. Sellers sell their business at a premium price (often more than their original asking price) when they offer a buyer very advantageous financing. A reduced down payment also expands the potential buyer market and lowers the buyer's risk—which in either case justifies a higher price.

5) **Financing.** Advantageous financing can outweigh price in importance. Astute buyers consider both financing and price because the two together determine what they ultimately pay for the business.

High interest rates depress business prices in the same way they soften demand for real estate, automobiles and other expensive consumer items. The cost of a 12

> *note* — A higher price is justified if the seller offers lower-than-market financing.

percent, 10 year, $100,000 loan is considerably more expensive than the same loan at 8 percent. Some buyers feel that if the interest on financing exceeds the prime rate, the excess should be deducted from the price. If financing is available below prime, the interest savings may be added to the price.

note — Interest affects price. Cash flow can be even more important. The loan period also influences the price as buyers rightfully limit the price to what the business can afford from its cash flow.

6) **Existing Profitability.** Valuation must largely relate to the future profitability of the business. However, price must also relate to present profitability. An enterprise with profits in place justifies a higher price than one in which the buyer must achieve those same profits.

Many sellers attempt to sell marginal or losing operations highlighting the potential of the business with the right buyer. While buyers buy potential, why should the buyer pay the seller for what the buyer will produce? Buyers should not. At best, the seller may be entitled to nominal goodwill—perhaps one year's anticipated profit.

Conversely, the business may already be at its top-earnings potential with no realistic way to improve upon its performance. Here, the buyer can only hope to maintain sales and profits. While the seller can demand a price that reflects those profits, the buyer should more conservatively value the business because the business lacks further potential.

Experienced buyers agree that the best acquisition is one that is operating far below its true potential, can be acquired at a low price and rapidly turned around. Such buyers typically pay slightly more than what the business is worth by strict valuation standards, yet get a bargain when the business fully blooms.

How to value the insolvent company

Insolvent businesses are commonly acquired for rehabilitation under bankruptcy, receivership or foreclosure. The turnaround potential motivates the acquisition, but its future profitability is not the chief criteria for determining its value. Buyers of these troubled businesses approach valuations from the seller's perspective—which is to liquidate the assets at auction. If

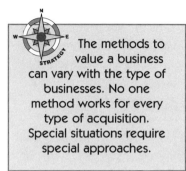

The methods to value a business can vary with the type of businesses. No one method works for every type of acquisition. Special situations require special approaches.

other interested buyers bid for the business, the competition bolsters the price. However, each buyer will use liquidation value as the basis for negotiating.

A buyer offered an insolvent business not yet under formal insolvency proceedings may find that the seller arbitrarily set the price to what he needs to liquidate his debts. This asking price, of course, bears no relationship to the actual value of the business.

The proper approach would be for the seller to undergo insolvency proceedings and allow the buyer to acquire the business at liquidation. As an incentive to the seller, the buyer would pay the seller personal compensation in the form of a covenant-not-to-compete, a share of future profits or perhaps only the opportunity for employment.

Valuing the service business

Service businesses—such as professional practices and brokerage firms—usually have few tangible assets. They chiefly sell their existing accounts and customer lists assets. The difficulty in valuing this type of goodwill is that sales and goodwill are so closely tied to the relationship between the seller and her customers. With the business or practice sold, these customers may discontinue patronage.

The traditional approach when valuing the service business is to set a price as a percentage of future sales from the existing customers. Tangible assets may be valued separately.

This percentage will depend on industry custom, but is generally between 15 and 35 percent of sales for three to five years. Patronage beyond that is due to the new goodwill created by the buyer. There are instances in which the buyer will acquire the accounts and customer lists for a fixed price. However, even then the price must be based on the anticipated future sales.

Valuing the merged business

When the acquired business will be dismantled and functionally merged into the buyer's business, the buyer cannot base its value on the profitability of the business intact, but must instead translate the economic benefit of the merger on his present income statement.

> **HOT spot** The seller who agrees to payment from future sales must concern himself with the ability of the buyer to retain goodwill and maximize the sales on which payment is based.

This exercise requires a careful analysis of each of the operational changes that will arise from the merger and an equally careful reconstruction of the buyer's pro forma profit-and-loss statement. The functional merger may synergize the buyer's profits and create combined profits considerably greater than the profits of the two separate organizations.

The functional merger and synergized profits may justify a higher value than would be justified from operating the acquired company separately, and this benefit to the buyer should enter into the price negotiations.

Protecting the buyer

Chapter 8

Protecting the buyer

What you'll find in this chapter:

- ⮕ Warranties that protect the buyer
- ⮕ Protection from a seller's creditors
- ⮕ Covenants pending the closing
- ⮕ Conditions to a buyer's performance
- ⮕ The Covenant Not to Compete

Chapter 5 discussed the procedures for investigating the legal affairs of the business, which is only a preliminary procedure to assess potential legal pitfalls. This earlier legal investigation does not protect the buyer. The buyer only gains legal protection from comprehensive contractual safeguards and the opportunity for recourse against the seller should later legal complications materialize.

Essential warranties to protect the buyer

To protect the buyer, the seller must give specific warranties and representations on which the buyer can rely to acquire the business, which are then made part of the contract.

Warranties, covenants and representations each have a different legal purpose. *Warranties* may extend to both present or future circumstances. *Representations* apply only to existing facts. *Covenants* are representations or warranties, concerning acts the seller agrees to subsequently perform. The distinction is important in the contract.

In an asset transfer, the principal warranties and representations come from the seller. If the seller is a corporation (usually liquidated shortly after the sale), a warranty from the selling corporation cannot adequately protect the buyer because the corporation will have no assets and the buyer no recourse. The stockholders of the seller corporation must then be personally bound on the warranties, representations and covenants of the selling corporation.

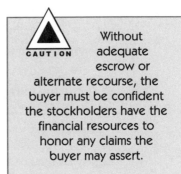

With a number of stockholders, the buyer must secure their joint and several representations. One problem is that the stock ownership may not be equal among the stockholders, and the selling stockholders may accept liability proportionate to their stock ownership. Minority stockholders are commonly passive investors and may not be personally familiar with the affairs of the corporation or able to confidently guarantee management's warranties.

Warranties

The buyer usually obtains financial statements from the seller. However, even certified statements do not guarantee accuracy. The buyer must, even with certified statements, obtain the seller's express warranty that the statements are complete and materially accurate in all respects.

Tax returns may be substituted for financial statements. The warranty should then also acknowledge they are true copies. Tax returns do not detail balance sheet items as thoroughly as financial statements and should not be used in their place when buying corporate shares.

 While financial warranties are always important, it is less essential on asset transfers, especially when the buyer shall acquire only specified assets and does not rely on the seller profitability or sales history to buy the business.

Financial warranties do not replace specific representations concerning certain assets, nor do they adequately warrant such items as liabilities and contracts which must be warranted separately under the agreement.

Accounts receivable warranties

When accounts receivable are sold, the buyer needs warranties as to their collectability. The agreement should annex the acquired receivables and represent that they arose in the ordinary course of business and are without known defenses, setoffs or counterclaims.

HOT spot The buyer should not be required to undertake litigation to collect the receivables. Conversely, the buyer should not be allowed to adjust or compromise a receivable if the buyer expects reimbursement from the seller for the uncollected balance.

Another important safeguard is a seller warranty that the receivables are collectable in due course. Essentially, the receivables are then sold on recourse. The agreement may provide, for example, that should any receivable not be fully collected within 60 days (or some other specified time), the uncollected receivable shall then revert to the seller who will promptly reimburse the buyer.

If the intent of the parties is to allow the buyer to adjust or compromise receivables while preserving his rights against the seller, the agreement should specifically reserve that right, and the buyer should give prior notice to the seller and an opportunity for the seller to object to the proposed settlement.

The seller should insist that payments on any accounts receivable be credited first to the oldest balance—or the transferred receivables rather than the new receivables generated by the buyer. If the seller must re-acquire uncollected receivables, the agreement also may impose some restrictions on the seller's collection methods. Excessive collection tactics can injure the goodwill purchased by the buyer.

Inventory warranties

The price for the business may be based on a stipulated inventory at closing. Any change to inventory will adjust the price.

How is the inventory to be valued? Various formulas can be used, depending largely on the type of business. Some contracts use a last-in, first-out or first-in, first-out method. Still others use prevailing replacement values, including all generally available trade and cash discounts. The retail trades commonly use a formula that discounts, from the retail price, the normal markup on each merchandise category.

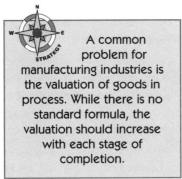

A common problem for manufacturing industries is the valuation of goods in process. While there is no standard formula, the valuation should increase with each stage of completion.

Another problem is that of excluded inventory. The buyer would want the agreement to specify that only marketable goods suitable for resale are to be included in the inventory valuation. In no event should the parties rely on prior markdowns or reserves for obsolescence as reflected in the seller's financials because these markdowns are frequently excessive to reduce for taxes. Still, some inventory may have questionable value and a fractional or discounted value can be assigned to these items. Alternatively, the seller may remove or exclude these from the sale.

Inventory valuations, even when well-defined, can cause numerous conflicts between buyer and seller. This conflict can usually be avoided by designating an independent inventory firm to tabulate the inventory following the valuation formula set within the agreement. The tabulator's determination would then be binding upon both parties, who would equally pay their fee. Every industry has commercial inventory tabulators, and it is best to select one experienced within the industry who can be impartial, and with no prior affiliations with either party.

A seller's warranty that the inventory at closing will be within a set range is another important, but commonly overlooked, warranty for the buyer. Without this warranty, a seller may deplete the inventory before the closing. Although the depletion will correspondingly lower the price, the seller who liquidates inventory gains more upfront cash and has less to finance.

Conversely, the seller should not be allowed to build excessive inventory. For example, a seller may attempt to unload on the buyer undesirable inventory from affiliated companies. A minimum-maximum inventory warranty should also prevent the seller from buying or disposing of goods, other than in the ordinary course of business. The seller also should be required to maintain a normal inventory mix.

> HINT The buyer who anticipates a higher inventory is faced with a cash flow problem because of the immediate need to replace inventory.

Contract warranties

If the buyer is to assume the seller's outstanding contracts, the agreement should warrant these contracts. The agreements should specify those contracts and recite that the contracts are in full force on their stated terms and are not in default.

In an asset sale, the seller should warrant that the contracts are either assignable, or that the seller will use her best efforts to obtain their assignment. Instead, this may be a condition precedent or subsequent to the sale, with a stipulated price adjustment if an assignment of a contract cannot be obtained despite the seller's best efforts.

If a lease or essential contract is to be assigned, the buyer should not rely solely on the seller's representation, but should obtain direct verification that the lease or contract is in good standing through an estoppel letter.

Tangible assets warranties

Significant tangible assets—such as major equipment, machinery, computers and office furniture—should be scheduled by the parties and included in the contract. Frequently, buyers find items have been removed by the seller before the closing. Important intangibles such as patents, copyrights and trademarks also should be scheduled.

HOT **spot** Items that are not owned by the seller (such as items on the premises under loan or lease) should also be expressly listed. The seller should expressly disclaim title to these items.

The warranty on assets to be sold should further specify their working condition at the time of the sale. A buyer may insist on good working order at time of the sale, or the parties may agree that the items shall be in the same working condition as on the contract date. The parties should then schedule any existing defects to avoid disagreement about when the defect occurred.

Liabilities warranties

Assets are generally acquired free and clear of all liabilities. If the buyer is to assume the seller's liabilities, the agreement should specifically list those liabilities.

Similarly on stock transfers, the buyer should not rely on the aggregate liabilities contained on the seller's balance sheet. The buyer is entitled to absolute protection from any unscheduled liability, and a broad warranty and indemnification is required to insulate the buyer from any unlisted liability—whether secured or unsecured, absolute or contingent, accrued or payable at a future date, and notwithstanding whether the seller is primarily or secondarily liable. The warranty and indemnity also should extend to any claim asserted by any creditor for an amount above that scheduled to be assumed by the buyer.

note

The indemnified liabilities require careful draftsmanship. For example, will it cover continuing obligations to service goods sold under a warranty policy? What if the buyer defaults on the timely delivery of goods on an order previously accepted by the seller? Are insured claims covered?

The seller asked to indemnify against potential liabilities will have several concerns: Is his potential risk under the indemnity disproportionate to what his benefits are from the sale? For example, a seller who is to net $30,000 from the sale may consider it unwise to indemnify against a possible $100,000 claim. The limits of liability under the seller's indemnity are often tied to the seller's net benefit or the buyer's investment.

Other drafting items to consider:

- Is the indemnity issued in consideration of the sale, which allows the buyer to rescind in the event of default?

- Does the indemnity protect the buyer from liability or loss? With a liability agreement the seller must intervene and save harmless or protect the buyer from any asserted claim. Indemnification based on loss only allows the buyer to reimbursement after he pays the indemnified claim.

- Does the indemnity insure the seller notice of any asserted claim so the seller can intervene and defend? The notice provision should specify how and when notice is to be made.

- Does the indemnity provide remedies to the buyer if the seller refuses or fails to defend? Can the buyer defend on her own? Is she authorized to settle or compromise undefended claims and still obtain reimbursement?

- What if the creditor obtains a pre-judgment attachment against the business on a defended claim? Can the buyer demand to be saved harmless from this attachment?

- Does the indemnity cover ancillary costs? Is the buyer entitled to recover legal costs on defended claims or to enforce the indemnity?

- Is the indemnity for a limited dollar amount per claim or for aggregate amounts? Does it contain a time limitation?

- Is there adequate security for the indemnity? Are funds escrowed? Can the buyer setoff against notes owed the seller?

The obvious complexity of these issues illustrates why an asset transfer is usually preferred over a stock transfer.

Qualifications and authority warranties

The seller also must warranty the corporation, its authorities and the assets or shares of stock to be sold.

Standard warranties concerning the corporation are that:

◆ The corporation is a valid entity and in good standing.

◆ The corporation is qualified as a foreign corporation (if applicable).

◆ The financial statements submitted to the buyer (or annexed to the agreement) are complete, accurate and fairly present the corporation's financial position and the results of its operation.

- The authorized capital shares of the corporation are as stated, and the outstanding shares have been lawfully issued and are fully paid and nonassessable, and there are no outstanding options, demands, subscriptions or warrants for any further shares.

- That the corporation has good and marketable title to all assets or property on its premises (or as annexed on a schedule).

- That there are no liabilities existing other than those contained within the financial statements (or as annexed on a schedule).

- That no material adverse changes have occurred in the business of the selling corporation since the date of the financial statement (or excepting such changes as are reflected on an annexed amended statement or schedule).

- That no material adverse change has occurred in the corporation's financial condition since the date of the financial statements (or excepting such changes as are reflected on an annexed amended statement or schedule).

- That the only executory contracts or leases to which the corporation is a party are those listed on an annexed schedule, and all said contracts are in full force without modification or default.

- That since the date of the financial statements, there have been no dividend payment or declaration, nor any distribution of any kind with respect to the seller's stock, nor any purchase, redemption or other acquisition of the seller's stock.

- That since the date of the financial statements, there has been no general increases in compensation of directors, employees or agents except in conformity with the corporation's established compensation structure or arrangements.

◆ That there are no liens, encumbrances, security agreements or attachments on any asset or properties of the corporation (or except for those annexed and scheduled).

◆ There are no known tax audits presently pending against the corporation by any government agency.

◆ There are no known condemnation proceedings, foreclosures, evictions or any proceeding in the nature thereof that would impair the future tenancy of the corporation under its lease.

◆ There are no known labor relations or collective bargaining efforts pending or contemplated against the corporation.

◆ That there are no known legal suits, to which the corporation is a party (except for those scheduled).

◆ There are no known criminal, civil, or administrative proceedings existing or threatened against the corporation by any governmental body or agency (except for those scheduled).

◆ The corporation holds all required licenses and permits to conduct its business, that they are current and in good standing, and that there are no known proceedings to revoke, cancel or suspend same.

◆ The corporation maintains, and will continue to maintain, adequate insurance pending the closing.

◆ The corporation does not maintain with its employees any contractual bonus, deferred compensation, retirement, pension or other similar arrangements (except as scheduled).

◆ The corporation is duly authorized to enter into the agreement and conclude the transaction and that all requisite stockholder and director votes have been obtained and certified as such by due corporate resolution. Further, the signatory to the agreement and any closing documents are fully authorized and there are known proceedings or litigation, actual or threatened, to enjoin or otherwise impair the seller's obligations under the agreement.

◆ Each of the foregoing warranties and representations shall continue in full force and effect, or if there is any material or adverse change, such change shall be stated in writing to buyer prior to closing and this agreement shall then be voidable at buyer's election.

◆ All warranties and representations shall survive the closing (except for those specifically stated not to survive the closing). On a stock transfer, certain additional warranties should be made by the selling stockholder, which warranties relate to the subject shares:

- the seller has good and marketable title to the shares to be sold

- the shares constitute percent of the outstanding shares of said corporation, all classes inclusive

- the shares are fully paid and are nonassessable

- the shares are free of any lien, encumbrance or pledge and upon transfer the buyer shall have good and marketable title

- there are no outstanding proxies or assignment of rights attaching to said shares

- there are no restrictions on transfer against said shares (or that any restriction has been duly waived) and that seller has full right and authority to sell and transfer said shares

- upon any stock split, or grant of preemptive rights or warrant pending closing, buyer shall be entitled to said additional shares under any split and/or an assignment of rights on any warrants

- on a sale of assets, the buyer will be less interested in the representations concerning the seller corporation, and instead need specific warranties to ensure the passage of good title to the acquired assets. These warranties are that:

  - the seller has good and marketable title to all assets to be sold (except for non-owned items scheduled)

  - the assets are to be sold free and clear of all liens, encumbrances, attachments and claims of all creditors, or any other adverse claim (except for specified assumed liabilities)

  - upon sale, the seller shall tender to the buyer a warranty bill of sale

  - the assets are to be sold in good working order (or in their present condition but without warranty of merchantability)

Depending upon the nature of the transaction, the condition of the seller's business and its financial condition, other warranties and representations may be required. The foregoing, while common representations and warranties, are not necessarily complete or satisfactory for all circumstances.

Protecting the buyer from the seller's creditors

Since most small business transfers are asset sales, the assets must be sold free of claims by the seller's secured creditors, general unsecured creditors, and any taxing authorities.

Secured liabilities

Creditors with validly perfected secured liens have an absolute right to recover the secured assets transferred to a buyer or any other third party. Secured transactions under Article 9 of the Uniform Commercial Code include all contractual arrangements in which personal property (tangible and intangible) serves as collateral security. A security interest includes chattel mortgages, factors liens, conditional sales agreements (and lease/purchase options construed as conditional sales), trust deeds, equipment trusts, trust receipts, and consignment sales, as well as assignment or transfer of chattel paper, contracts and accounts receivable.

The initial step in investigating secured claims is to determine whether any such claims have been duly perfected. Secured creditors must strictly adhere to the requirements for perfecting their security interest under the Uniform Commercial Code, as enacted within the debtor's state.

 Many states require recording in both a state office and the town or county where the debtor (seller) is located. In these circumstances, the buyer may erroneously check only the town (or county) filings without searching the state filings. Moreover, the seller may have conducted its business in two or more towns thus requiring only a state filing. Owing to the ever existing possibility of a faulty search, a commercial search firm should be used as a double check.

A common error when conducting a security interest search is the failure to search under all names, for example, when the seller operates under an assumed or trade name. Frequently, a search will uncover a security interest more than five years old and technically lapsed. In other situations, the filing may be only in one public office although additional filings are required. Or the description of the collateral arguably may not include assets to be transferred.

While it is beyond the scope of this book to cover the technicalities of secured transactions, the essential point is that the buyer's counsel must ascertain that all security interests are properly terminated at the time of sale—including those of questionable validity. The agreement should require the buyer to deliver all termination statements at closing, although the buyer or seller may be allowed to pay these debts from the proceeds of the sale.

Federal tax claims

The seller's balance sheet may show outstanding tax liabilities. Even when they do not, it is important that the assets are purchased free of tax liens or possibility of transferee liability for the sellers known or contingent tax claims.

Under the Internal Revenue code, a bona-fide purchaser for value accepts the assets free of federal tax claims owed by the seller, unless a lien is recorded or the buyer expressly agrees to assume the seller's federal tax liability. Assuming the buyer bargains to acquire the assets free of tax claims, she must verify there are no tax liens. The search should include both the public offices where security interests are filed and the federal district court in the seller's jurisdictional district. If real estate is acquired, the search should include the deeds registry.

> *note* The IRS can only assert a claim for the amount stated on the lien plus interest and statutory additions. But the IRS only reluctantly discharges a lien when all other non-liened tax liabilities are paid.

There are several practical problems with a federal tax lien. One is that the lien may have been fully paid but remain undischarged. As with security interests, this is quite common, as many taxpayers neglect to obtain a tax lien discharge upon payment. As an alternative, the buyer can conclude the purchase but escrow an amount for the face amount of the outstanding tax lien.

State tax claims

The states often impose a harsher rule than the IRS concerning transferee liability for unpaid taxes. Massachusetts, for example, and many other states, impose transferee liability even when no tax lien has been filed. The effect is to make the buyer secondarily liable for all state taxes owed by the seller even when the buyer has no public notice of these tax claims.

To avoid transferee liability in these states, the seller must provide the buyer tax waivers, certificates of good standing or other documents commonly issued by the state taxing authorities to acknowledge full payment of taxes and to bar future state tax claims against the buyer. In all states, a discharge of state tax liens must be obtained.

Municipal tax claims

A less likely problem are municipal tax claims. Generally, these are excise taxes on personal property; however, like state taxes, municipalities may impose transferee liability even when there is no lien.

Unsecured liabilities

Early in the transaction, the buyer should approximate the seller's unsecured liabilities to see whether or not the debts can be fully paid from the sale. If the liabilities exceed the assets, leaving unliquidated debts, then the buyer must follow the procedures for acquiring the insolvent business as discussed in Chapter 13. In other instances, the buyer should comply with the Bulk Sales Act.

 The Bulk Sales Act, in effect in most states, requires the buyer to notify all of the seller's creditors of the intended sale no less than ten days before the sale. If the buyer fails to do so, the seller's creditors can later make a claim against the assets sold to the buyer.

The principal question for the buyers' counsel should be whether compliance with the Bulk Sales Act (Article 6, UCC) is necessary, or can the buyer safely waive its cumbersome requirements and instead rely on other safeguards? The answer depends on two factors:

1) Will the debts be fully paid from the sale's proceeds?

2) Will the buyer have certain, efficient and practical recourse against the seller should a creditor claim arise later?

Before waiving the Bulk Sales Act, the buyer should insist upon six contract provisions:

1) That the seller provides the buyer an affidavit listing all creditors (including those that are disputed or contingent). This discourages a seller from intentionally eliminating major disputed creditors, to conceal the business's insolvency.

2) That the buyer can pay all liabilities from the sale's proceeds. No funds should be released to the seller until all claims have been paid and each creditor acknowledges full payment.

3) That the buyer escrow part of the sales proceeds to satisfy later claims. While this is negotiable, it is common for the buyer to escrow as much as one-half the listed liabilities for six months (the period within which creditors must file claims).

4) That principals of the selling corporation indemnify the buyer from any asserted claims. Notwithstanding other safeguards, only an absolute and secure indemnity justifies a Bulk Sales waiver.

5) That there be a set-off provision within any notes due the seller as recourse for any claim. This safeguard alone does not justify a waiver because the buyer may be forced to immediately pay claims, and only have the right to set-off against future installments. This, of course, may seriously impair the buyer's cash flow.

6) That the buyer obtain a comfort letter from the seller's counsel acknowledging that counsel is unaware of any unlisted liabilities, lawsuits or other pending or contingent claims. The attorney does not warrant that such liabilities do not exist but only that counsel has no knowledge of their existence.

> Unless the risk from waiving the Bulk Sales Act is small, the buyer should comply, particularly if the buyer is to make a large investment in the business.

Strict compliance with the Bulk Sales Act insulates the buyer from transferee liability. Its provisions are reasonably uniform among the states and the principal steps to comply are:

- The seller prepares an affidavit listing his liabilities.

- The buyer gives the listed creditors notice of the intended bulk transfer.

- The notice is to be received by the creditors at least 10 days before the sale and delivered either personally or by registered mail.

- The notice must, as a statutory minimum, state: (a) that a bulk transfer is intended, (b) name and address of the seller and buyers, and all other business names and addresses used by the seller during the preceding three years and (c) whether or not all the debts of the seller are to be paid as they fall due. If the transferee is uncertain on that point, then the notice shall further state (d) the location and general description of the assets to be transferred and the estimated total of the seller's debts, (e) the address where the property is located and may be inspected, (f) whether the transfer is for new consideration, (g) the time and place of payment and (e) the time and place for creditors to file their claim.

- The buyer is to preserve the list and schedule for six months following the transfer, which creditors may inspect during reasonable working hours.

Non-action by creditors within the 10 day notice period constitutes an assent by the creditors who no longer can maintain a claim against the transferred assets. State laws differ whether the buyer has a legal obligation to distribute or ensure the distribution of proceeds from the sale to creditors. However, it is recommended that the parties escrow payment to ensure creditor assent for the sale.

Covenants pending the closing

To protect the buyer's interest in the business, between the agreement date and closing, the agreement should contain several affirmative and negative covenants. These usually serve three broad purposes:

1) To prevent a material or adverse change in the operation of the business or its financial or legal affairs.

2) To allow the buyer to examine or become involved in the affairs of the business and thus ensure a smooth transition.

3) To obligate the seller to perform all conditions required to close on the transaction.

One alternative to covenants is to defer signing the agreement until the closing. A simultaneous signing and closing avoids the typical buyer's concerns that "bad things will happen to the business" before the closing. The obvious disadvantage with this is that the sale may collapse at the last moment.

The seller's affirmative covenants may include:

note Affirmative covenants compel the seller to perform certain acts. Negative covenants prevent certain acts by the seller.

- *Rights to examine books.* The seller covenants to provide the buyer full access to its records, contracts, books and other internal documents to help ensure an orderly transition.

- *Rights to hold required meetings.* Securing appropriate votes or resolutions to enter into the agreement and conclude the sale should be accomplished before signing the agreement. However, when further votes are required, obtaining these votes should be a covenant to be performed before the closing.

- *Rights to secure assignments.* During the transitional stage the seller should secure all required consents to assign or transfer leases, contracts and other rights, including insurance—if the buyer shall assume these contracts.

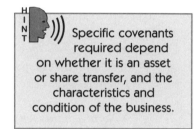 Specific covenants required depend on whether it is an asset or share transfer, and the characteristics and condition of the business.

- *Conduct of seller's business.* The seller should covenant to conduct the business in the normal course and to take all reasonable steps to preserve the goodwill for the benefit of the buyer. Specific provisions may require the seller to maintain

  ◆ business hours

  ◆ prices

  ◆ service policies

  ◆ credit policies

  ◆ sales and advertising efforts

- *Maintenance of assets.* The seller agrees to maintain inventory within defined limits, and repair or replace machinery or equipment as reasonably required.

- *Obtain tax ruling.* If a tax-free transaction is contemplated, it is usually the seller's obligation to secure the tax ruling. This may be either a condition or covenant pending closing.

- *Obtain "no action" letter from SEC.* If the transaction is exempt from registration under the Securities Act of 1933, it may be a condition of sale to secure a "no action" letter from the SEC confirming the exemption. The obligation to secure this is the seller's.

The seller's negative covenants include operational constraints designed to prevent dissipation of the assets or goodwill. Typical negative covenants are:

- ◆ *No increased indebtedness.* The seller may not materially increase the debts of the company or incur new debt, except in the ordinary course of business.

- ◆ *No new mortgage.* A specific covenant should prevent new mortgages or security interests on business assets.

- ◆ *No extraordinary contracts.* The seller may not enter into any contracts or commitments, except in the ordinary course of business.

- ◆ *No extraordinary capital expenditures.* The seller shall not make any capital expenditures or additions, except those reasonably required to maintain equipment or the physical plant.

- ◆ *No contractual terminations or modifications.* The seller shall not terminate or modify any existing contracts or leases that are to be assumed by the buyer.

- ◆ *No employee terminations.* If the buyer intends to employ the seller's employees, a covenant should prevent their discharge or termination unless for good cause. A reciprocal provision may require the seller to obtain the buyer's approval for hiring new employees during the transition.

♦ *No new compensation programs.* This covenant prevents the seller from increasing or changing compensation programs, including bonuses, pension benefits, fringe benefits or severance.

♦ *No distribution, issue or redemptions.* The seller will not declare or pay any dividend or make any other distribution upon its shares and shall not purchase, retire or redeem any of its outstanding shares. The seller also should agree not to issue any new shares or change the ownership or capital structure of the selling entity.

♦ *No charter or by-law amendment.* The seller should agree not to alter or amend the charter or bylaws except as may be defined within the agreement.

Conditions to buyer's performance

Conditions precedent are those conditions upon which the buyer's obligations to perform are expressly subject. Without these conditions precedent, the buyer would be in breach of his agreement if he did not buy, even though satisfaction of the conditions are necessary for the buyer to perform.

There are many possible conditions and whenever possible they should be satisfied prior to agreement. However, a buyer should never assume she can satisfy a condition and therefore exclude it from the agreement.

A buyer, for instance, may make his commitment to buy the business conditional upon:

• **Financing.** If financing is required to conclude the transaction, obtaining that defined financing should be a condition of purchase.

• **Leases.** Assent to assignment by the lessor of the present lease, or obtaining a new acceptable lease, is a commonly cited condition.

- **Compliance with seller's covenants.** Full compliance by the seller of each of the seller's stated affirmative and negative covenants may be reincorporated as a condition for closing. Upon any breach by the seller, the buyer should have the additional rights to damages.

- **License transfers.** All required transfers of licenses and permits should be made a condition. If the transfer cannot occur until after closing, the license transfers should be made a condition subsequent, rather than a condition precedent, to closing.

- **Contract assignments.** If important contracts, franchise agreements and similar contract rights are to be assigned, the agreement should be conditional upon approval of the assignment.

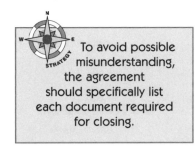

To avoid possible misunderstanding, the agreement should specifically list each document required for closing.

- **No material loss or casualty.** Closing should be conditional upon no intervening casualty loss, even if covered by insurance. Minor losses may be excluded provided the seller is obligated to repair or replace.

- **No unfavorable administrative rulings.** The buyer's obligation to buy should be conditional upon obtaining favorable rulings by the IRS, SEC, Federal Trade Commission and other agencies with jurisdiction over the transfer.

- **No material customer changes.** If the seller depends upon certain key customers, the continuity of their business relationships should be a condition of purchase. Termination of business by important customers must be carefully considered when acquiring any business.

- **Adverse material change in financial condition.** The agreement should be conditional upon no material change in sales, assets or liabilities before closing. Considerable care must be used to draft this. A broad clause will be resisted by the seller, and an over-restrictive clause will work against the buyer. When possible, specified ratio limits and other quantifiable parameters should be used.

- **Accounts certification.** If the closing is subject to a specified financial condition, the agreement should contain the further condition that the seller's accountant verifies that financial condition.

- **Delivery of documents.** Typically, the agreement is conditional upon the seller providing, at closing, certain documents and side agreements to be signed by others not a party to the original agreement. This may include releases, indemnity agreements and nondisclosure agreements. Additionally, the seller may need to execute or deliver certain documents such as corporate and financial records, assignments, bills of sale and other standard closing documents. Execution and delivery of each document would be a condition of closing.

- **Opinion of counsel.** The buyer should not be obligated to close unless he receives a satisfactory opinion from the seller's counsel that represents that all proceedings and actions required by law or the terms of the agreement have been taken and satisfied, and that all required administrative opinions and authorizations have been secured.

The Covenant Not to Compete

Unlike covenants to be performed before the closing, the Covenant Not to Compete is to be performed subsequent to closing. In terms of protecting the goodwill acquired by the buyer, this covenant remains the most important post-closing agreement, whether the sale is for assets or stock. There are six essential points when negotiating the noncompete agreement:

1) ***Parties.*** If the seller is a corporation, the noncompete agreement should be signed by the corporate entity as well as its principals. Since its objective is to prevent active competition, it is only necessary to secure the agreement of the principals actively engaged in the business. Inactive stockholders may be excluded.

Obtaining a non-compete agreement from key managers or technical personnel also is important. This, however, is often difficult to obtain since employees do not benefit from the sale. They generally join in the noncompete only as a condition for future employment with the buyer.

The covenant should bind and benefit not only the buyer and seller but also their successors or assigns. Because the covenant is a valuable asset, its assignability should be expressly stated.

2) ***Consideration.*** The parties should expressly state the amount paid for the covenant to distinguish its consideration from the consideration for the acquisition. The IRS may otherwise allocate a substantial part of the purchase price to the covenant and tax it as ordinary income. The buyer may want to allocate goodwill payment to the covenant so the buyer can deduct the noncompete payments as an ordinary business expense. The allocation must be negotiated, however nominal consideration is usually allocated to the covenant.

3) ***Restricted activity.*** The heart of the agreement is the restricted activity which should prevent the seller from directly or indirectly engaging in any business materially or substantially competitive with the business to be sold, notwithstanding whether the seller (or its principals) is the owner, principal, partner, officer, director,

note To preserve the business' trade secrets, the noncompete also should impose nondisclosure and confidentiality constraints on the seller.

agent, employee, consultant or stockholder (except a minority stockholder of publicly owned corporations). Another restriction is to bar any direct or indirect solicitation of, or providing competitive goods or services to, any existing or future customer.

No matter how carefully the restriction is drafted, problems do arise. For example, does the agreement prevent employment within a competitive company if the seller is assigned to a noncompeting division or subsidiary? What if the seller is employed by a noncompeting company that later competes? Is the seller then obligated to quit or only obligated to restrict his duties to  noncompetitive activities? Or what activities or products are considered competitive with that of the business to be sold, particularly when the business expands its products or markets?

A buyer should negotiate the broadest possible geographical protection.

4) *Geographic constraints.* Most agreements impose geographic constraints or boundaries within which the seller may not compete. The courts will not enforce an agreement that is geographically unreasonable as they will not prevent a seller's gainful employment absent a showing it is reasonably necessary to protect the goodwill sold to the buyer.

When you are determining geographic reasonableness, the courts will consider existing markets and future markets that are reasonably foreseeable at the time of agreement. Therefore, the buyer should recite within the agreement its projected or planned markets to justify a broad geographical constraint. Even if it is considered unreasonable, a court will not nullify the contract but only reduce the geographical radius to what it considers reasonable.

Another difficulty with a geographical limitation is that it typically bars competition within a certain radius of the present business address. What then are the rights and obligations of the parties if the business relocates or expands to new locations?

5) *Time constraints.* As with geographic constraints, the court also will enjoin competition only for a reasonable time. The courts will consider customer turnover, the unique characteristics of the business and even its purchase price. Ten-year covenants are generally enforceable. Longer covenants may be upheld when unique skills are involved.

6) *Remedies for breach.* The remedies for breach should be carefully outlined. It is reasonable to have a notice and cure provision in the agreement in the event of an alleged breach, so the seller has the opportunity to challenge a contested activity without risking a greater damage claim from a continued breach.

While the buyer will normally have both injunctive (equitable relief) and a claim for monetary damages arising from a breach of the noncompete, the agreement should provide that injunctive relief is available without posting bond. If seller financing is involved, the noncompete agreement may provide set-off rights in the event of breach. However, these rights as well as the rights of rescission may nevertheless exist as a matter of law.

Financing the acquisition

Chapter 9

Financing the acquisition

Correctly financing the acquisition is critical to both the seller and buyer. Some sellers view financing as only the buyer's problem and insist on an "all-cash" sale. They overlook the importance of financing in the buy-sell process and fail to work with the buyer to shape the financing that can best serve their respective needs. The net result is that the business stagnates on the market and forces the seller to negotiate with endless prospects before one is found with the required cash. More often, in desperation, the business is sold at a bargain price.

HOT spot The future success of the acquired business is influenced—if not controlled—by its financing.

Financing is seen by the seller as a way to get paid for the business. For the buyer, financing must mean considerably more. More businesses fail because of improper financing than most other factors. Improper financing also restricts growth, creates tax problems and even causes conflicts between partners.

Financing centers on seven key questions:

1) How much capital is needed?

2) How should the invested capital be divided between borrowed and owner funds?

3) Are partners preferable to borrowing—and if so, what is a fair partnership deal?

4) What are the best sources for acquisition financing?

5) How do you apply for a business loan?

6) What terms should be negotiated?

7) How should the loan be structured?

 Accountants and attorneys may have some experience arranging financing for their clients. Their specialty and prior financing involvements with other clients determine their usefulness as financing advisors.

Business finance is not a simple subject. As with valuations, it is a specialty and poses complexities that may be beyond the buyer and his advisors. This chapter does not cover all the intricacies of financing, but instead highlights the key points. There are many excellent texts on small-business financing.

Types of financing

Financing the small business acquisition usually comes from three primary sources:

1) **Internal Financing.** That part of the sales price that is financed by the seller, through the assumption of debt or similar financing

opportunities that exist within the business and are made available to the buyer.

2) **External Financing.** Funds borrowed from external sources— such as banks, SBICs, and similar lenders.

3) **Equity.** The amount invested by the buyer.

The buyer must first investigate the available internal financing for only then can he estimate the capital that must come through other sources, including his own personal funds.

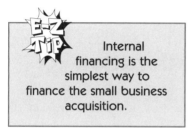

Internal financing is the simplest way to finance the small business acquisition.

Consider, for example, the business selling for $100,000. The buyer without internal financing has a $100,000 problem. However, if the buyer negotiates a $70,000 loan from the seller and assumes $10,000 in trade debt, the buyer suddenly reduced the problem to only $20,000.

Financing must go beyond what is required to buy the business. The buyer also must forecast the working capital needed to ensure fiscal stability and to grow the enterprise. Buyers who overlook this point mistakenly approach financing as a two-step process. They first exhaust their capital or borrowing power to buy the business and later look for financing to build their business. They are usually unsuccessful because their collateral is already pledged and the original financing cannot be reshaped to accommodate additional financing. A buyer should incorporate working capital into the initial financing.

note More businesses are financed through seller financing— or by the buyer assuming debts of the seller—than are financed from outside capital sources.

A buyer should closely examine the balance sheet to see what assets and liabilities can release cash and reduce the need for outside financing. Excess inventory, for example, may be partially liquidated. If the buyer will not assume the seller's debts, the cash

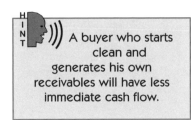

A buyer who starts clean and generates his own receivables will have less immediate cash flow.

flow projections should reflect this as available credit. Buying the seller's receivables affects financing because receivables creates an immediate income stream.

The debt/equity allocation

The buyer also must determine how to allocate financing between external debt and equity. For many buyers, the answer is decided by their own limited funds. Whether or not preferred, leverage is the only way these buyers can afford to buy. The well-capitalized buyer must determine whether or not to use more or less of his own funds.

Leverage is the trend in small-business acquisitions. Buyers prefer to invest as little of their own money as possible. This can be seen even with large-business acquisitions. About half of all such acquisitions are made with an equity investment of five percent or less. More than 95 percent is debt financing. Why is this so? There are three reasons:

1) **Risk.** Buyers are, and should be, risk oriented. Invested capital is capital at risk—a discomforting thought few buyers overlook. Even though these same buyers may be personally liable on the financing, they gain some protection because the loans are collateralized with business assets. The buyer's liability is then limited to any deficiency should the business fail.

2) **Reserve capital.** No matter how carefully the capitalization requirements are forecasted, a business inevitably demands

additional capital. Leverage allows the cash-shy buyer to retain a contingency fund for these unanticipated costs.

3) **Tax advantages.** Interest payments on borrowed funds are tax deductible. This is of considerable importance to the business with significant profits.

These are only a few advantages to maximum financing. The decision to borrow heavily also may be motivated by the desire to invest excess funds in other ventures.

> **note** Fast-growth companies often owe their spectacular—but often shaky—growth to their ability to buy with razor-thin investments.

Leverage frightens more conservative accountants who want a more sizeable equity investment to avoid the dangers of under capitalization and the inability to pay what they see as excess debt. This possibility, however, exists even with the better-capitalized company that never manages to earn quite enough to pay their loans.

Preparing the loan proposal

The importance of the well-prepared loan proposal to successful financing is apparent. Most loan applications are refused only because they fail to provide the lender sufficient information to justify the loan. Large corporations understand the need for a well-documented loan proposal, but buyers seeking capital to buy the smaller firm too often approach a lender as if they were seeking a car loan or a home mortgage.

Preparing a well-documented loan proposal is not difficult. Most of the information and documentation will have been gathered during the evaluation stage and only requires logical compilation to give the lender the information he will need on five main points:

1) **Credit and Personal History**

   - name and address
   - marital status
   - employment history
   - education
   - personal assets and liabilities
   - military status
   - bank references
   - credit references
   - outstanding lawsuits

2) **Business History**

   - name and address of business
   - narrative description of business
   - history and age of business
   - financial statements for prior three years
   - tax returns for past three years
   - summary of proposed business changes
   - capital needed for improvements
   - pro-forma balance sheet (three years)
   - pro-forma income statement (three years)
   - pro-forma cash flow statement (three years)
   - lease or proposed lease terms

3) **Terms of Sale**

   - sales price
   - method of transfer

- buyer's investment and source of funds

- other financing and terms

- date of proposed purchase

- copies of letter of intent or agreement

4) **Collateral for the Loan**

- description and listing of major business assets

- acquisition or replacement cost of assets

- liquidation value of assets

- insurability of collateral

- financial statements of guarantors

5) **Proposed Loan**

- amount of loan

- loan period

- interest

- guarantors to loan

- collateral

- other loan terms

- date for loan approval

A lender will assess each item following the traditional three C's of credit:

1) The lender must be satisfied that the applicant is *creditworthy*.

2) The business has adequate *cash flow* to repay the loan.

3) The *collateral* to be pledged will adequately secure the loan.

Some lenders look primarily for strong management, but others are more concerned with the stability of earnings. Asset-based lenders rely mostly on collateral. The way lenders prioritize each factor can vary.

All lenders want a successful venture because that is the only way their loan can be repaid. Lenders decline loans when they see fundamental defects in the acquisition or the long-term planning for the business. The lender's opinion on the acquisition is indeed valuable and the lender's expertise essentially makes him part of the acquisition team.

Still, not all pessimistic lenders are correct. Lenders, like everyone else, find their hindsight is considerably more accurate than their foresight. Nevertheless, buyers should carefully weigh the reasons a loan is refused. There may be an important message that has been overlooked.

Sources of financing

Finance books discuss the many possible sources of financing. The scarcity of loan sources for small businesses partly explains the popularity of seller financing. It is not that seller financing is always desirable, but rather that it may be the only financing obtainable. And, as many small business buyers have discovered, the only other likely lenders are relatives and friends.

> *note* Small business buyers have comparatively few sources to choose from, and each of these lenders are asset-based and rely primarily on tangible collateral for the loan.

Small businesses (with sales less than $2 million annually or requiring an acquisition loan less than $200,000), should consider commercial banks or SEA guaranteed loans. These two sources account for about 85 percent of all external debt funding. But there are other sources:

Banks

As stated, commercial banks are the primary lenders for small-business acquisitions. As asset-based lenders, they limit their loans to the liquidation value of the pledged assets. However, more aggressive banks will lend more than the liquidation values of the collateral if the acquired business has a strong record of earnings and proven management. For more speculative loans, the bank also may want a pledge of personal assets, such as a home or securities, and the bank may increase their loan to reflect the value of these personal assets.

 Selecting the right bank is important. Start with the seller's bank because it is most familiar with the business. Prefer local banks over distant banks, since local banks are community-oriented and know local market conditions. The bank also will expect to be used as the depository bank, so it must be convenient to the business.

SBA business loans

The Small Business Administration offers a variety of loans to start, acquire or expand a U.S. business. Buyers who are unsuccessful with direct bank borrowing should consider SBA financing as their next alternative.

There is one very discouraging reason why SBA loans are not widely used for business acquisitions: The SBA needs two to six months to approve a loan, and few sellers will give the buyer that much time to get financing. This is a most important point for a seller to bear in mind if the sale is conditional upon SBA financing.

note The SBA will sometimes make direct loans rather than participatory loans for businesses in depressed locations.

SBA loans are through local banks. The prerequisite is that two banks must first refuse the loan. The SBA will then guarantee the bank loan and surcharge the loan 1/2 percent as payment for the guarantee. The SBA guarantee is limited to 90 percent of the loan, so the risk is shared 90/10 between the SBA and the participating bank which directly loans the funds and administers the loan.

The SBA loan offers one important advantage over bank financing: SBA loans can be repaid over seven to ten years. Bank loans typically have a five-year maturity. The longer payback can greatly ease cash flow.

Aside from the slightly higher interest and the inevitable SBA delays, the SBA loan signals one other problem: the SBA finances only more speculative and risky loans that banks refuse. The fact that a business cannot qualify for bank financing signifies perceived risk in the acquisition and signals a need for caution.

Commercial loan companies

Larger acquisitions requiring more than $500,000 rely more on nationwide commercial companies such as Walter E. Heller & Co., James Tolcott Business Finance, Aetna Business Credit, ITT and Commercial Credit Business Loans.

Because commercial loan companies handle larger loans, they are generally more flexible than banks in designing the right loan package. This flexibility allows these firms to finance leveraged buyouts or higher risk deals that are unacceptable to banks.

For the increased risks, these firms charge 3 to 8 percent higher interest than banks, demand closer control over the business and may even bargain for an equity interest in the business. Their equity participation is usually less than with Small Business Investment Companies (SBICs) and venture capital groups, as commercial loan companies view themselves primarily as lenders while venture capitalists are equity oriented.

Factoring firms

If accounts receivable is the primary asset of the business, the buyer should consider factoring. For instance, New York's Meinhard-Commercial lends up to 85 percent against current receivables. Banks, on the other hand, may limit their loans to 50-60 percent of the receivables. The buyer usually gains borrowing leverage by pledging the tangible assets to a bank while factoring the receivables.

Even if a factoring is not necessary to fund the acquisition, it can help cash flow after the acquisition and should enter the buyer's financial planning. The purchase and sales agreement should then be conditional upon obtaining both the acquisition financing and factoring commitment.

Leasing firms

The equipment-intensive business may utilize any one of a burgeoning number of leasing firms, such as Equico Leasing. As equipment-oriented lenders, they finance more against capital assets. Alternatively, the buyer may sell the acquired equipment to these firms and then lease it back.

How to negotiate the loan

A buyer may necessarily shop several prospective lenders before she finds her best loan. Aside from testing the loan market, the buyer will benefit from the many divergent opinions about the acquisition.

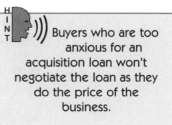

HINT: Buyers who are too anxious for an acquisition loan won't negotiate the loan as they do the price of the business.

The buyer's accountant and attorney should assist in the loan negotiations. They are usually more familiar with commercial borrowing. The negotiation checklist should cover five principal points:

1) Amount to be financed

- Does the borrowed amount cover the capital needed for the acquisition and the working capital?

- Will the buyer be allowed an additional line of credit above the initial amount borrowed?

- Will the additional lines of credit be secured or unsecured? Will it be at the same or a different interest rate?

- Can the buyer refinance up to the original amount once the loan balance decreases?

2) Interest

- Is the interest rate adjustable or fixed?

- If the interest rate is adjustable, does it have a "cap" and a "floor," or upper and lower range?

- How is the prime rate determined? Does the lender have lower or higher prime rates than other lenders ? Is interest tied to the average floating prime charged by other selected banks?

- How often is the interest adjusted?

- Will interest be reduced as the loan balance decreases?

- Is the interest competitive with rates charged by other lenders?

- Will the loan require the payment of "points," loan fees, or origination fees?

3) *Term of loan*

- Is the term sufficiently long for the loan to be paid from the projected cash flow?

- Is the loan automatically renewable, and on what terms?

4) *Payment schedule*

- Are payments made monthly or quarterly?

- Is the loan on a direct reduction basis as to principal payments?

- For a renewable loan, which amortization schedule will apply to the principal during the original term? Which amortization on the extended terms?

5) *Collateral*

- What collateral must be pledged for the loan?

- Will the lender release the collateral or subordinate its security on the collateral upon reduction of the loan? What are the terms and conditions for release or subordinations?

- Is the buyer required to maintain collateral at defined levels?

- If accounts receivable are to be financed, which receivables qualify? What is their loan value? What is the hold-back for bad debt?

- What guarantors are required for the loan? Will the guarantees be absolute or limited?

- Are the guarantors obligated to pledge personal assets? Will these assets be released upon reduction of the loan balance?

How to structure the loan

Properly structuring the loan is critical. The loan should be made by the lender directly to the acquiring entity as the primary obligor. The principal of the acquiring entity will ordinarily guarantee the obligation and may pledge personal assets to support the loan.

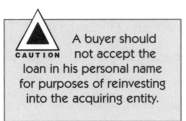

A buyer should not accept the loan in his personal name for purposes of reinvesting into the acquiring entity.

With the acquiring corporation as the borrower, the lender will mortgage the business assets, thus shielding the principal from a deficiency on the loan should the business fail. The ability to grant the lender a business mortgage and protect the buyer can only be accomplished this way.

The buyer's accountant and attorney also must decide how to apportion the owner's investment between debt and equity. A more highly leveraged acquisition may create a "thinly capitalized corporation" under the Internal Revenue Code. Certain states set their own minimal equity capitalization. A more conservative buyer may want a 20/80 or 30/70 equity/debt ratio.

The buyer's attorney should carefully document the loan from the principal to his acquiring corporation. To withstand IRS scrutiny, a promissory note with interest at or above 10 percent, to be repaid within a reasonable time, should be prepared. The principal also should invest the equity funds one or two months before the loan so that the debt will not be construed as an equity contribution.

HOT spot Many acquisitions are doomed to fail because no effort was made to evaluate the business' capacity to handle its loans.

The safest way for the principal to loan to her own corporation is to pledge a passbook or securities to the lender as additional security. The lender will then increase its loan against the business for that amount. Structured this way, the principal's loan is protected by the same business collateral that secures the lender's original loan. The principal can not obtain this same protection by directly lending to her own corporation on a secured basis, because stockholder or "insider" loans can be set aside and subordinated to the claims of arms-length creditors should the business go bankrupt.

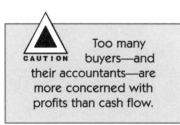

Too many buyers—and their accountants—are more concerned with profits than cash flow.

Before the financing is in place, the buyer and his accountant measure the business' capability to pay back loans. The one vital role of the buyer's accountant is to see that the "numbers work" and the business can pay—and with a reasonable margin of safety.

The buyer should project cash flow for at least the first two years of the loans. Financing often may extend five years or more, but projecting cash flow that far into the future becomes too speculative to be meaningful.

Financing needs cautious projections. A buyer may optimistically work backwards and inflate projected sales to conveniently cover what is needed to pay the debt. When the projections prove faulty, the buyer is left with the alternative of collapsing the business, modifying the debt through agreement, a reorganization proceeding, investing further equity capital from personal funds or taking in partners. Regardless of the remedy selected, it pinpoints poor financial planning.

Preparing the purchase agreement

10

Chapter 10

Preparing the
purchase agreement

The sales contract accomplishes considerably more than just reducing to writing what the parties have agreed upon. Corporate, tax, financing and other important legal issues overlooked during preliminary negotiations must now be resolved. Many of the less obvious terms and conditions essential to a well-conceived sale are never discussed or even considered before writing the contract, so there is seldom a true meeting of the minds until there is a signed agreement.

A vague contract only invites disputes and protracted litigation.

The agreement is usually prepared initially by the buyer's counsel because the buyer needs the broader protection. The parties should identify and resolve all foreseeable issues in advance so the contract serves as a written recitation of terms rather than a platform for further negotiation. As with all contracts, the parties' counsel must foresee the numerous contingencies and problems that may occur and provide appropriate remedies.

The parties may forego the contract altogether when there is an imminent closing, but this is not recommended. A contract provides structure to the transaction and instills safeguards beyond what can be provided by the bill of sale and other closing documents.

Contracts for the sale of assets

Asset transfers are the most common type of transaction for the smaller firm. Most of the provisions found in asset sales also are contained in contracts for other types of transactions and are therefore included only in this discussion of asset sales.

Here are 17 essential points for asset contracts:

1) Parties

The agreement should include all parties to the agreement. Beyond the corporate seller and buyer, the principals of the respective entities should join in the agreement to the extent they will be personally bound on indemnifications, notes, covenants, noncompete agreements, guarantees and other undertakings. If the transaction involves business brokers or finders, they should assent to the commission. If other signatories to the transaction are required, they too should execute the agreement to bind their performance, rather than rely on obtaining their signatures at closing.

> Parties to the agreement should note their involvement as "their respective interests exist and are represented," to reflect limitations on their involvement.

2) Recitals

Recitals are not binding provisions but are important to portray the general intent of the parties. While not all-encompassing, recitals characterize the nature of the transaction, such as if the business is sold as a "going concern" and if there is to be a total ownership change. Recitals also are important to clear ambiguities in the agreement's intended effect and therefore must be carefully drafted to reflect that intent.

3) Assets to be sold

The contract must accurately specify all assets to be sold. Many disputes center on this. Seldom will the transaction involve all assets of the business, thus it is essential to carefully delineate assets to be sold from those to be retained by the seller. A comprehensive list of assets to be categorized include:

- cash on hand

- accounts receivable

- notes receivable

- securities or interest in other entities

- prepaid deposits and utilities

- tax rebates

- insurance claims

- litigation claims and chases in-action

- inventory

- furniture and fixtures

- equipment

- motor vehicles

- leasehold improvements

- real estate

- goodwill

- business name

- patents

- trademarks

- copyrights

- customer lists

- trade secrets

- licenses and permits

- transfer of telephone numbers

On asset transfers, the seller usually retains liquid assets such as cash, receivables, prepaid expenses and securities. Real estate also may be retained as it is often owned personally by the principal of the seller's entity. In many instances, the sale includes nothing more than transferring inventory, furniture, fixtures, equipment, name, and goodwill, although the division of assets always is the essence of the agreement.

 A detailed description of each asset to be sold should be annexed as an exhibit. However, if all assets within a category are sold, it is important to recite that a specific item listing is not all inclusive, as individual items may be overlooked. An individualized item listing applies to major assets—such as equipment and motor vehicles.

4) *Assets to be retained*

Listing the assets to be sold implicitly defines the items to be retained; nevertheless, it is best to specifically list the retained items. Beyond listing categories of retained assets, the list may include specific items within a category otherwise scheduled to be sold. For example, the seller may sell furniture and fixtures, while retaining

note The asset-retention clause also may include other assets not otherwise scheduled to be sold.

certain office furniture for future personal use. Or perhaps one automobile will be retained while vehicles generally will be sold.

5) *Excluded items*

Certain items used in the business may not be owned by the seller and thus are neither sold nor retained. These are items loaned or leased to the business, consigned goods and similar items subject to reclamation by third parties. It also may include certain leasehold improvements such as carpeting, air conditioning and other items attached to the real estate and that must remain with the landlord upon termination of the tenancy.

Delineating these non-owned items is necessary to disclaim any implied warranty of title. If possible, the seller should preserve his rights to return these items even prior to the closing unless the buyer made his own arrangements directly with its owner for continued possession of the non-owned item.

6) *Purchase price*

The purchase price may be set as a:

DEFINITION

- *Fixed price.* Here the purchase price is a fixed-dollar amount established prior to the contract.

- *Formula price.* This contemplates the payment of a fixed price and this amount is not ascertainable before closing. An example: A price based upon actual inventory, receivables or assumed liabilities at time of closing. This also may be treated as a fixed price subject to adjustment. Here, the contract should clearly specify the formula for establishing the price and methods for determining the amount or value of each item upon which the formula is based.

DEFINITION

- *Contingent price.* This is determined entirely or partially on the basis of future earnings (often called an earn-out) for a specified formula period following the closing. The price is paid at stated intervals during, or at the end of, that period. A contingent price must be drafted carefully to define the method of computation and the seller's rights to an accounting to determine compliance. The contingent price also may be coupled with a fixed or formula price.

7) *Payment of purchase price*

The price may be paid by:

DEFINITION

♦ *Lump-sum payment.* This contemplates the payment of the total purchase price (less deposits) upon closing.

♦ *Installment payment.* This provides for the payment of the price in installments. With a formula price, the parties must stipulate if the adjustments will alter the down payment or the amount to be financed. When it changes only the amount financed, the contract should specify if it increases the number of installments or the payments per installment.

The contract should define the financing terms including the installment period, interest, notes to evidence the debt, guarantees to the note and each form of collateral security for the note. Each financing document should be prepared at the time of contract and appended as exhibits to avoid later disputes over the financing document terms.

HOT spot Funds payable at closing should be cash, certified check or bank check. Deposits paid before closing would be a credit against the down payment.

If the buyer's principal office is out of town, the seller should require payment in local clearing house funds, thereby avoiding clearance delay. The agreement also may provide for escrow of the closing documents pending clearance of the down payment.

The deposit should be sufficient to commit the buyer and may call for additional deposits as the conditions precedent to the transaction are satisfied.

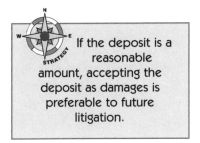

If the deposit is a reasonable amount, accepting the deposit as damages is preferable to future litigation.

Brokers often hold the deposit, although in the absence of brokers or an escrow bank, the attorney for the buyer or even both counsel, may hold the deposit. The escrow agents should be signatories to the agreement, or issue an escrow letter stating their obligations to release the escrowed deposit, and the procedures to be followed in the event of a dispute. The parties should stipulate if the buyer will forfeit all or part of the deposit as liquidated damages in the event of breach of contract.

8) *Allocation of price*

The allocation of the purchase price among the various acquired assets is required for tax purposes. The buyer will attempt to allocate as much of the price as possible to the depreciable assets to gain a high beginning basis. This may be contested by the seller who may realize a taxable capital gain if the assets have been substantially depreciated. However, in most instances, the seller will plan either a three-month or twelve-month liquidation, thus treating the entire transaction as one taxable event to the stockholders of the selling entity.

The allocation has more than tax significance. If a value is fixed for a particular asset and the asset is subject to misrepresentation, the allocated price may be decisive in determining damages. Insurance companies also may base loss-claims on the allocated amount.

HINT Allocated assets should equal the total purchase price and include assumed liabilities when the assumed liabilities are a part of the purchase price.

9) *Liabilities*

If the assets are intended to be sold free and clear of all of the seller's liabilities, the agreement should so specify. Buyers will want to take all required steps to protect themselves from trailing liabilities. This may include the contract requirement to comply with the Bulk Sales Act, indemnifications from the seller and its principals, the right of offset against notes due the seller, escrow of proceeds or a combination.

Contracts usually allow the seller to use the price proceeds to discharge liens or encumbrances. Here, the buyer will coordinate payment with receipt of the appropriate discharges. This includes all tax waivers and other documents necessary to ensure clear title.

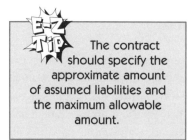

The contract should specify the approximate amount of assumed liabilities and the maximum allowable amount.

Liabilities may be assumed by the buyer and credited toward the purchase price. While the precise liabilities to be assumed are usually unknown at the time of contract, the contract may define the liabilities by aging or categorization. At the time of closing, the seller will provide the actual liabilities to be assumed which may be incorporated as part of the contract.

If liabilities are to be assumed, the buyer may reserve the right to compromise or settle these liabilities, without subsequent price adjustment, provided that the compromise does not create residual liability to the seller. This is a desirable provision when the liabilities are excessive.

The seller will want reciprocal protection on assumed liabilities. This should include indemnification from the buyer entity and its principals. The contract also may require payment within a specified time and proof of payment. Also, the seller may require security agreements, a pledge of the shares of the buyer entity or other collateral to insure the buyer's performance.

The parties may elect a split approach: the buyer may assume certain liabilities and the seller others. The seller may want to pay those liabilities on which the principals are personally liable—such as guaranteed debts and tax obligations. The contract must then state if the seller or buyer will thereafter select the liabilities to be assumed.

10) *Representations and warranties*

Representations and warranties are contained within the contract and the contract should provide that the warranties survive the closing. Since warranties may form the basis for a later claim of misrepresentation and fraud, the preamble should provide that each warranty is material and relied upon by the other party for purposes of entering into the transaction.

If the seller is a corporation with negligible assets, its principals should join in the warranty. If the stock ownership is unequal, the agreement may allocate liability so that each stockholder's interest is proportionate to her ownership interest.

Seller's warranties

A comprehensive checklist of possible seller warranties include:

- seller has good and marketable title

- assets are sold free and clear of liens and encumbrances

- seller has full authority to sell and transfer the assets

- seller, as a corporate entity, is in good standing

- seller's financial statements present fairly and accurately the financial position of the company as of its date, and there are no material adverse changes thereafter

- contract rights and leases to be assigned are as represented and in good standing

- there is no material litigation pending against the company

- all licenses and permits required to conduct the business are in good standing

- there are no liabilities other than as represented

- the seller's name does not constitute an infringing use on the name of any other entity

The parties may warrant certain assets to be sold. For example, the seller may warrant inventory levels or collectable accounts receivable at closing. The seller cannot know in advance the precise value at the closing and therefore the warranty may be limited to a prescribed value range.

HOT spot If the warranty extends to certain documents such as financial statements, tax returns, leases, and assigned contracts, these documents should be defined within the warranty for identification, with copies attached.

The agreement should further specify those warranties which are not intended to survive the closing and are deemed satisfied upon closing. The buyer will ordinarily insist that all warranties survive the closing except for those subject to validation at the time of closing. An example of the latter: A warranty that the equipment is in good working order.

Buyer's warranties

In a cash acquisition, the buyer's warranties are generally limited to those concerning its existence and authority to consummate the transactions contemplated under the contract. If the seller provides financing, the warranty will extend to representations about the buyer's financial condition.

A well-drafted agreement will incorporate warranties from the buyer to protect the seller if the transaction is not consummated. The buyer may warrant it will not use the seller's trade secrets, induce employees to leave and that confidential information will stay confidential. To ensure that the buyer will not compete with the seller if the transaction is canceled, the buyer may covenant not to compete with the seller. The protective warranties also may stipulate that the buyer will not enter into a lease for the premises except in an acquisition.

Definition:

Covenant Not To Compete. A contractual term or condition to guarantee one party will refrain from conducting business or professional activities similar in nature to another party's.

11) Conditions

DEFINITION

Conditions make performance conditional upon certain events and reciprocally allow for avoiding the closing if the conditions are not satisfied. Unlike warranties and affirmative or negative covenants which are generally within the control of the parties, conditions are ordinarily non-controllable and depend on third party actions. Again the distinction is narrow, and what one contract may treat as a condition another may consider a warranty or affirmative obligation.

Most conditions are imposed by the buyer. Essentially, buyers must consider every occurrence upon which the transaction should or must depend. A representative checklist includes:

♦ All of the seller's warranties and representations shall remain accurate and true at the date of closing.

♦ There have been no materially adverse changes in the seller's financial performance prior to closing.

♦ The seller provides all required documents contemplated by the agreement, at the time of the closing.

♦ All required opinion letters have been obtained.

♦ An assignment of lease, or new lease on terms acceptable to buyer has been obtained.

- Satisfactory financing for the transaction has been obtained.

- Approval by governmental agencies (if required) has been obtained.

- Licenses and permits can be transferred.

This list, of course, exemplifies only the more common conditions. The many possible conditions are limited only by the foresight of the respective parties and their counsel.

note

Vague, poorly drafted conditions serve only as "escape clauses" for a buyer seeking to terminate the contract. Therefore, the conditions must be both reasonable and sufficiently specific to determine whether it was or was not satisfied. For example, a condition for financing on terms satisfactory to the buyer allows the buyer the opportunity to arbitrarily avoid performance by rejecting even the most favorable financing. A preferred approach is to specify the financing terms. Or, the contract may require the respective parties to expend "best efforts" to satisfy the conditions. While this imposes an affirmative obligation, it nevertheless is subjective and encourages litigation.

If the contract imposes conditions in which the seller has no control (financing, satisfactory lease, etc.) the seller must assess the likelihood the buyer can satisfy the conditions. The seller should set a defined time period for the buyer to satisfy the conditions. On that date, the buyer should be contractually obligated to either confirm satisfaction of all conditions or terminate the contract with a return of the deposit. The parties may agree to extend the date for performance, but this is usually done by contract amendment when the conditions are not fully satisfied by the contract date.

> **The seller's position should not change in anticipation of a sale until all conditions have been satisfied.**

The buyer must be certain the conditions are satisfied prior to acknowledging the satisfaction. For example, a lender may verbally agree to finance or a landlord to a new lease and later rescind their agreement. The buyer who relies on a non-binding, third party contract to acknowledge satisfaction of the condition nevertheless stands in breach to the seller when he cannot perform.

Infrequently, there will be conditions subsequent to the closing. Ordinarily these conditions cannot be satisfied prior to the closing. A common example is the transfer of licenses through a licensing agency if a prior sale is required. With conditions concurrent, the agreement generally provides that the sale is subject to rescission if the conditions are unsatisfied. This imposes a considerably greater burden on the seller. The buyer is operating the business and without the necessary safeguards, it may be impractical to put the parties in their status quo position.

Due diligence in satisfying subsequent conditions certainly are a requisite. The contract also may provide for joint administration of the business during this interim period.

12) Covenants

DEFINITION

Covenants may be either affirmative or negative and include mandatory and prohibited acts by either party pending the closing or thereafter. Most covenants are performed by the seller and relate to the operation of the business pending closing. These covenants are designed to prevent the seller from harming the goodwill or adversely affecting the financial or legal structure. Small business covenants may deal with the maintenance of business hours, inventory, credit and service policies, pricing, and other operational items essential for customer retention.

Negative covenants during the transition period customarily have the same desired objective of prohibiting acts that would diminish goodwill or somehow impair the buyer. In the negative covenants, a seller may agree not to terminate key employees without cause, disrupt favorable relationships with customers or disclose trade secrets to others. Many of these transitional safeguards also may be expressed as warranties and their full compliance also would be a condition of closing.

Specific language should be used when drafting the affirmative and negative covenants to be observed during the preclosing period. Many agreements simply recite "the seller will undertake all acts reasonably required to maintain goodwill." Although broad verbiage is useful, it becomes valuable only when coupled with more definitive prohibitions. Even when the seller is dealing in "good faith," a particular act may be viewed as incidental to winding down her business affairs and yet the buyer may view it as destructive to the goodwill of the business.

> **HOT spot** As either warranties or covenants, a breach allows for a damage claim, while its concurrent status as a condition also would excuse the buyer from performance.

Disagreements do occur during the transitional period, so the buyer will want all possible protective clauses. The seller should reciprocally insist on a notice requirement and "right to cure" if there is an alleged breach of a preclosing covenant. Also the seller will want a provision acknowledging that acceptance by the buyer of the seller's bill of sale constitutes conclusive evidence of full performance of the seller's preclosing covenants and responsibilities. This stipulation is vital to the seller as there are numerous instances of a buyer closing on a transaction and later complaining of a seller's preclosing breach of contract. This is a common tactic when the buyer wants to escape paying the seller's note.

> The closing documents, when detailed, have a practical as well as legal importance. The parties may then rely on the listing to prepare for the closing and eliminate delays.

Covenants also will apply to acts performed at closing. Normally, the agreement will specify the respective documents to be delivered by the buyer and seller, which extends not only to closing documents but also to the delivery of specified books and records regarding the conduct of the business.

In drafting the Covenant Not To Complete, the agreement will incorporate all the parties—including employees—expected to execute the covenant, and they should sign the agreement. It is also best to prepare separate covenants for each party, even if the terms are identical. As separate and divisible contracts, a breach by one party will not constitute a breach by the others.

The covenant should specifically state its consideration, even if nominal. Absence of stated consideration may allocate a portion of the goodwill toward the covenant. The covenant should also be specific as to prohibited acts and impose reasonable time and geographic constraints. The remedies for breach

HOT spot The Covenant Not To Complete is the most important post-closing covenant. Its importance in the buy-sell process may allow it to stand as a separate item within the contract.

should also be carefully defined. As with preclosing covenants, the seller may want notice of breach and an opportunity to cure. Thereafter, the buyer will want injunctive relief without posting bond, in addition to legal remedies for damages. The covenant also may stipulate whether or not the buyer will have the right to delay or set-off payments due the seller on a purchase money note. Reciprocally, the seller should be released from the covenant upon default under his note obligations from the buyer.

13) Casualty

DEFINITION

The contract must contemplate the possibility of casualty to the assets before closing. A common provision is for the seller to maintain adequate insurance. Upon casualty, the buyer either assigns the claim to the buyer, or the buyer terminates the agreement. *Minor casualty*, defined as casualty to assets comprising less than 10 percent of the aggregate value of the assets to be sold, may be an exception. Here, the buyer should be limited either to accept the insurance proceeds or accept a price adjustment. The seller also may have the right to replace the asset.

Casualty to the premises should give the buyer the same rights as a casualty to assets. If the casualty terminates the lease or causes minor business

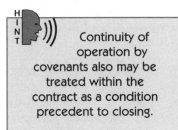

Continuity of operation by covenants also may be treated within the contract as a condition precedent to closing.

interruption, the parties may agree to extend the closing for a reasonable time to allow the seller to restore the premises to its prior condition.

If the business is within a shopping center or depends on a nearby business for traffic, the buyer should extend the casualty provision to other tenants or the shopping center itself. This allows the buyer to either terminate the contract or defer closing until the designated premises or co-tenant have resumed operation.

14) Brokers

Brokers or finders due commissions should become parties to the agreement to confirm the commission arrangement and their obligations as escrow agents if they hold deposits.

Often cobrokers are involved. One broker provided the business listing and the other the buyer. Ordinarily the division of commissions is decided between the cobrokers by agreement. The cobroker also should join in the agreement to confirm commission participation.

While brokers are entitled to a commission upon producing a buyer ready, willing and able to buy on the offered terms or such substitute terms as the seller may accept, the seller should condition payment to the brokers on an actual closing. This avoids a broker's claim against the seller if for any reason the sale is not concluded.

The contract should also provide for allocation of the deposit in the event of a buyer breach that results in deposit forfeiture. The broker also may bargain to participate in any recovery against the buyer for damages. Here, the agreement should set forth the proportion of recovery due each and apportionment of litigation costs.

The agreement should provide if the broker shall be a copayee on the note to reflect the broker's interest, or if the broker will simply accept the seller's note. In a seller's note to the broker, the payments may or may not be proportionate to the buyer's payments to the seller. However, the seller should at least make payments to the broker conditional upon receipt of payment from the buyer.

Many brokers who defer their commission prefer to enter into a direct financing arrangement with the buyer, with a corresponding reduction of the price payable to the seller. The broker may want a security interest against the business with priority over the seller's collateral, while the seller may want the broker to hold a subordinate mortgage. One practical resolution: the seller's and broker's security should be in parity.

> *note*
>
> Occasionally, where there is seller financing, the broker will defer part of the commission until receipt of payment by the seller.

If the buyer pays the seller directly, the seller should demand a release from the broker thus avoiding a liability if the buyer does not pay. If a release is absent, the seller should obtain indemnity from the buyer, which may include a security interest to enforce payment.

 Each broker document should be incorporated within the agreement as exhibits to be executed by each party at closing.

15) *Adjustments*

Most asset transfers require closing adjustments between seller and buyer at closing. Prior to drafting the agreement, counsel should review the allocable items with their respective clients, as the clients are most familiar with the operational items that may require adjustment. The agreement should identify each item to be adjusted and the adjustment formula.

The adjustments also should handle goods ordered by the seller prior to closing but received by the buyer after closing and therefore not tabulated in the inventory or price. The buyer should have the option to reject the goods or accept the goods as a postclosing adjustment.

note Common adjustment items include rent, payroll, insurance, utilities, service contracts, tax obligations, license and permit fees.

Typically, the parties will not be in receipt of all the final entries to adjust at closing. The contract may then provide for escrow of a part of the price to satisfy adjustments payable by the seller, and an escrow by the buyer to insure performance on his obligations.

16) *Miscellaneous provisions*

- *Incorporation of exhibits.* All documents identified within the agreement should be incorporated into the agreement by specific reference.

- *Jurisdiction.* If the buyer and seller are from diverse jurisdiction, the contract should stipulate the controlling jurisdiction for purposes of contract interpretation and enforcement.

- *Severability.* The severability provision allows the remaining agreement to survive, if one or more provisions are deemed unenforceable.

- *Survival.* The agreement should provide a survival clause that binds the parties' personal representatives, successors and assigns. Assignability may be allowed only to designate a nominee to accept title without releasing the obligations of the buyer.

- *Total contract.* A necessary provision is the clause disclaiming any warranties, representations, promises or inducements, other than contained within the contract. This prevents a subsequent claim of parole terms. This clause requires both parties to be certain the contract states the total agreement complete with all ancillary documents relied upon. The provision also may require amendments or modifications to be in executed form to avoid a later claim of verbal modification.

17) Closing date

The buyer and seller, typically anxious to close on the transaction, are often unrealistic in measuring the time required to complete the legal work, obtain financing and satisfy other conditions. The counsel's role is to set a realistic closing date and insure flexibility when the closing becomes extended for reasons beyond the control of either party.

Unquestionably, reasonable diligence should be used in closing as rapidly as possible, when that is the parties' objective. Because so many problems can develop before closing, the time should be shortened as much as possible.

On occasion, the parties will delay closing. For example, the parties may reach agreement in October but plan to close in January for tax purposes, or so the seller can benefit from the high selling season. Frequently, these concessions on closing date may greatly influence the price or other terms.

The parties also must decide if time is of the essence in closing the transaction or if either party shall have a reasonable time thereafter to perform. Strict performance is generally counterproductive because delays are common. The party demanding strict performance should offer valid reasons for the condition. Strict performance may apply to one party while the other reserves the right to extend as when one party has had prior delays and is offered one final extension.

> Unless strict performance is required for some compelling reason, it is best to build flexibility into the closing date and allow for an automatic extension of up to 30 days.

When scheduling a closing, select a convenient closing date. It is usually best to schedule the closing to coincide with a new business period—such as the first business day of a month—to easier calculate adjustment. Since a scheduled closing date is only a target, the parties should execute formal extensions when required.

Contracts for stock transfer

Many contract terms applicable to asset transfers apply to stock transfers and are not repeated here. Substantively, priorities become somewhat different. Asset transfers may be far less complex as the buyer's primary concern is that he obtain clear title to a business that is operating as represented with stock transfer, the buyer's priorities expand to include every facet of the corporate structure.

Model agreements show the diversity of clauses found in stock transfer agreements. However, essential to any stock transfer agreement are these eight points:

1) **Stock to be transferred.** The agreement must specify the precise stock interest to be transferred with these warranties relating to the shares of stock:

- The shares represent at closing, a stated percentage ownership of the corporation, all classes of stock inclusive.

- The seller has and shall deliver good title to said shares free of encumbrances, pledges or other liens.

- The shares are fully paid and nonassessable.

- There are no outstanding proxies or other assignment of voting rights.

- All restrictions on transfer imposed by the bylaws, or otherwise have been waived, allowing for transfer.

2) **Purchase price.** Shares of the closely held corporation are seldom sold for a fixed price. Generally, the formula price is used, adjusting for actual assets and liabilities at the time of closing. Although capital assets and goodwill may have a stipulated value, cash, accounts receivable, inventory and liabilities do change the value of the shares.

note As with asset transfers, the agreement must recite the method for valuing each at closing so the formula price may be determined.

Larger corporations are often sold for the book value at closing as based on audited financial statements. This has little application to the smaller firm whose assets, including goodwill, are typically valued as under an asset transfer.

3) **Warranties on the corporation.** The most important stock agreement provisions are these warranties concerning the legal, financial and business affairs of the corporation.

- The corporation is in good standing (and in all jurisdictions, if it is a foreign corporation).

- The corporation has good title to all the assets or properties used in connection with the business (except for those delineated as non-owned).

- All required federal and state tax returns have been filed, and all monies due were paid, and there are no known audits or notices of audit pending.

- All contracts (principal contracts to be specifically identified) are in good standing and not in default or threat of termination.

- All leases are in good standing, without modification or amendment.

- There are no known proceedings against the corporation by a governmental body or agency.

- The corporation is not a party to any litigation (except as may be delineated).

- There are no liens or encumbrances against any asset of the corporation (except as may be delineated).

- The corporation is not a party to any contract not subject to termination at will without penalty (except as may be delineated).

- The corporation has and shall maintain insurance (as specified).

- The corporation has no bonus, profitsharing, or pension plan (except as delineated).

◆ The financial statements annexed to the agreement accurately and fairly represent the financial conditions of the corporation as of its date, and there have been no material adverse changes since.

This list certainly is not all inclusive. Many other warranties can be included. The buyer's accountant and attorney should identify other warranties appropriate to the particular transaction, as considerable care should be taken to broadly protect the buyer.

The existing liabilities are usually scheduled by the seller as an exhibit to the contract. Unlisted or excessive liabilities are a breach of warranty and the remedies are normally indemnification, right to set-off against notes due the seller or claims for reimbursement. These conventional remedies may or may not preclude other remedies, such as rescission.

HOT spot Two very important additional warranties refer to liabilities and accounts receivable at closing.

"Liabilities" under the warranty must be carefully defined and should include the following: accounts payable, notes payable, expenses payable, taxes accrued to date, rent and occupancy costs accrued to date, loans due officers, directors, stockholders or any other third party, notes either secured or unsecured, accrued wages and any other debt or obligation, whether disputed or undisputed, liquidated or unliquidated, contingent or non-contingent and notwithstanding whether past due, current or due at a future time, and notwithstanding whether known or unknown.

The seller will equally want protection on indemnified liabilities covered by the warranty. The seller, for example, should have no liability for insured contingent liabilities. The seller may equally want to limit her liability to either the buyer's investment or the proceeds the seller derives from the sale. The limitations of liability remain an item for negotiation. At the very least, the seller will want notice of an indemnified liability and the right to defend and settle the liability before the buyer pays and seeks recourse against the seller.

The warranty on accounts receivable and other obligations due the corporation may be similarly handled. The closing documents generally schedule existing receivables, with a warranty for recourse against the seller if they are uncollected within a specified time. The buyer then conveys to the seller title to the uncollected receivables in exchange for repayment.

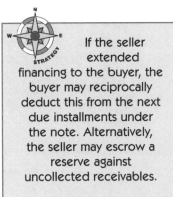

If the seller extended financing to the buyer, the buyer may reciprocally deduct this from the next due installments under the note. Alternatively, the seller may escrow a reserve against uncollected receivables.

The buyer will ordinarily rely upon certain inventories, liabilities and receivables—the formula price for the shares. It also is appropriate to warrant their acceptable range. A depleted inventory of receivables would reduce the purchase price but also the future cash flow of the business and the ability of the buyer to finance the acquisition.

4) **Covenants.** The affirmative and negative covenants under a stock transfer duplicate those found in asset transactions. In stock transfers, however, the covenants necessarily expand to protect the buyer from major changes in the corporation's financial or legal structure. Common additional covenants found in stock transfers include:

- *No new indebtedness.* The seller will not incur new debts, except for unsecured current liabilities in the course of ordinary business.

- *No new mortgages.* The seller will not incur any new mortgage, lien or encumbrance against the assets or convert unsecured debt to secured debt.

- *No extraordinary improvements.* The seller will not make any capital expenditures, additions or acquisitions except those required to maintain its property and equipment in a state of ordinary repair.

- *No extraordinary purchases.* The seller will not acquire additional inventory except in the ordinary course of business and as needed to maintain normal inventories.

- *No extraordinary disposition of assets.* The seller will not dispose of any of its assets, except for inventory in the ordinary course of business.

- *No defaults on contracts.* The seller will not default on any contractual obligations including the payment of secured debts, leases and similar obligations to be preserved for the buyer.

- *No extraordinary contracts.* The seller will not enter into any new contract of an extraordinary nature (to be defined in the agreement) which is to be performed after the closing without prior written consent of the buyer.

- *No distribution or redemption.* The seller will not declare or pay any dividend on, or make any other distribution upon its shares as of the contract date.

- *No assurance of new shares.* The seller will not make any changes in its capital structure.

- *No new compensation plans.* The seller will not pay any pension benefits (except those due) or severance pay or other bonus or compensation benefit to any officer, director or key personnel.

- *No charter or bylaw amendment.* The seller will not amend the bylaws, charter or articles of the organization, except in the manner expressly provided in the agreement.

- *Warranties to subsidiaries.* If the acquired corporation has subsidiaries, the seller will extend all warranties to each of its subsidiary corporations.

5) **Conditions.** Due to the many factors that may adversely affect the corporation to be acquired, the buyer may impose corresponding conditions for closing. The latitude of these conditions will largely depend on the parties respective bargaining positions. When the closing is not imminent, the buyer will require more protection from material changes which include:

- ◆ *No material adverse change in seller's legal, financial or business condition.* A material adverse change which substantially alters profitability, net worth or asset values should excuse the buyer from performance. Adverse legal factors include threatened or pending litigation not adequately insured against.

- ◆ *No material loss or casualty.* The corporation shall not have suffered any material loss as the result of casualty. However, the seller may have the option to replace the assets destroyed prior to closing.

- ◆ *No unfavorable administrative rulings.* The buyer's obligations should end unless it receives necessary or favorable rulings from the Internal Revenue Service, Securities and Exchange Commission or Federal Trade Commission or other agencies as stipulated within the contract.

- ◆ *No consents and assignments.* The agreement should be conditional upon the consent of any third party whose assent is essential to performance. This, for instance, may extend to lender consent when a loan obligation prevents a change of management or a franchise agreement stipulating the involvement of a named principal.

◆ *Releases and discharges.* The selling stockholder may condition the sale upon obtaining releases from personally guaranteed obligations, which may include the affirmative obligation of the buyer to guarantee the obligation.

◆ *No misrepresentations.* The representations and warranties given by the seller and all written statements delivered by the seller to the purchaser must be true, complete and accurate in all respects as of the closing.

◆ *Compliance with obligations.* The seller shall have fully performed each of its affirmative obligations and covenants and observed each of its negative obligations prior to closing. The seller may impose a reciprocal condition on the buyer relating to her own covenants.

◆ *Accountant's certification.* The buyer should not be obligated to perform if the financial statement of the seller at closing is not at least as favorable as that set forth in specified statements relied upon by the buyer to enter into the transaction. The condition is common in stock transfers of larger corporations in which the buyer may insist on a "cold comfort" letter at closing from the seller's accountant.

◆ *Opinion of counsel.* The buyer may condition performance upon receipt of an opinion from seller's counsel containing assurance that certain legal matters are in compliance. Generally, the opinion letter will extend to matters of corporate organization, pending litigation and assurance that all seller's covenants have been fully performed. The agreement should specify the particular assurance required in the opinion letter.

◆ *Discharge of personal debts.* One of the primary concerns of a selling stockholder in a stock transaction will be the objective to terminate personal liability on present or future corporate obligations. The seller's inability to discharge personally guaranteed obligations may necessitate an asset sale.

The selling stockholders may have personal liability to numerous corporate obligations. Often the seller is unaware of previously issued guarantees until long after the sale when the corporation is in default. The seller must identify the various obligations that require termination, novation or indemnification under the contract.

Any corporate obligations may be subject to guaranty. Loans due lending institutions invariably require the personal guarantees of the stockholders. Leases on the premises, equipment, or other long-term fixed obligations also may require personal guarantees.

It cannot be assumed that vendor obligations are without personal guarantees. Suppliers to the small business do demand guarantees, and in many instances, these guarantees have been issued years earlier when the business was first started. For this reason, the seller will want the contractual right to notify both present and past vendors that any existing personal guarantees are to be terminated for post-closing obligations. This should include personal guarantees on such commonly overlooked items as utility accounts, money orders, lotteries and fiduciary accounts.

The selling stockholder, as principal officer of the corporation, may also have statutory liability on corporate obligations—such as federal and state withholding taxes, sales and meal tax, unpaid payroll, and even unemployment compensation payments. These obligations may be handled in four ways:

1) ***Novation.*** The parties may have the creditor accept the buyer's guarantee in exchange for a buyer's release and can be accomplished when the buyer's and seller's credit standing is strong. If novation cannot be negotiated, the seller may insist the buyer join in the guarantee, and if possible, make the seller's guarantee secondary to the buyer's.

2) ***Prior payment.*** The seller may simply pay guaranteed obligations prior to closing.

3) ***Liability retention.*** The seller may pay the personally guaranteed debts directly, with a corresponding increase to the purchase price. The seller also may retain receivables or other assets for purposes of liquidating the debt.

4) ***Indemnification.*** If the seller is to remain bound on corporate obligations, the buyer (and its principals, if a corporation) can indemnify the seller. As with indemnifications for assumed liabilities in an asset transfer, the buyer should secure the indemnity.

What personally guaranteed debts can safely be left for the buyer? Secured debt adequately collateralized by business assets certainly imposes less risk than unsecured debt. The strength of the corporation and its ability to pay is another factor. If the debts are due soon or are payable over a long term when the business may be in decline is another consideration. Most significant is the strength of the buyer's indemnification.

> *note* The buyer cannot be expected to give a blanket indemnity for undisclosed debts. The burden is on the seller to discover all debts for which protection is required.

The contract must specify which obligations are subject to indemnification and which debts are subject to prior payment or payments from the sale proceeds.

6) **Releases.** Contracts customarily provide that the selling stockholder—and its officers and directors—release and discharge the corporation from all debts, contracts and other obligations existing at closing. If the corporation has loans due the seller, the release may constitute taxable income to the corporation as a forgiveness of debt. Any resulting tax liability must be adjusted between the seller and buyer. This, of course, would not apply if the corporation has a sufficient loss carryforward.

Conversely, the selling stockholder may owe the corporation for loans or other advances. The release between the corporation and the selling stockholder should then be reciprocal to avoid a later claim by the corporation now owned by the buyer.

7) **Delivery of documents.** Many side agreements are incidental to the purchase and sale contract. These include:

- Noncompete agreements

- Nondisclosure and secrecy agreements

- Employment contracts

- Indemnification agreements

- Financing agreements

- Escrow agreements

- Releases

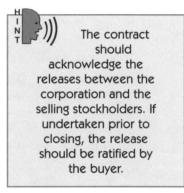 The contract should acknowledge the releases between the corporation and the selling stockholders. If undertaken prior to closing, the release should be ratified by the buyer.

These agreements are normally referenced within the purchase and sale contract and should be prepared in advance as exhibits. The execution and delivery of these agreements are then conditions precedent to the parties obligation to perform. The obligation to provide duly executed agreements is another affirmative covenant specifying damages in the event of breach, particularly when execution and delivery are within the seller's control.

8) **Finally,** the contract should make the buyer's obligation to perform conditional upon the delivery of various corporate records, data, documents and information including:

- Certificates of incorporation, bylaws, minute books, stock-transfer book and related corporate records.

- Resignation of the seller's officers and directors if requested by buyer.

- General releases from directors, officers and key employees of all claims against the corporation.

- Certified resolutions authorizing all corporate acts under the sale.

- Banking resolutions revoking prior authorizations and authorizing the buyer's full authority to corporation's bank accounts.

- All information in respect to the seller's products, processes, trade secrets and the seller's agreement not to use such information competitively.

- Corporate records, including contracts leases, insurance policies, supplier lists, customer lists, accounting records and computer software.

Handling nine special acquisitions

11

Chapter 11

Handling nine
special acquisitions

Several special situations offer their own unique considerations. This chapter deals with nine such transactions. Other special situations exist because transfers can be shaped in endless ways and are limited only by the participants' creativity, but only nine will be discussed here.

1) The franchised business

More than 40 percent of all small business transfers involve franchises. This is to be expected considering the rapid growth of franchising within the retail and service sector—both of which are a large segment of the small-business market.

At the outset, the buyer must decide if she wants a franchised business. The buyer may be motivated to buy a franchise because of its successful history; the support services or the reduced risk—all of which are considerable benefits. On the other hand, the buyer, as franchisee, must operate within strict operating guidelines—a prospect few true entrepreneurs are comfortable with.

HOT spot Franchising involves a unique relationship between the franchiser and the licensed franchisee so the acquisition necessarily becomes a three-way contract between buyer, seller and franchiser.

Few franchisers allow transfer of the franchised business without their prior approval. This restriction applies to both asset and stock transfers. By contract, the franchiser generally requires that the proposed buyer have the background and credit standing equivalent to new franchisees.

note The seller or buyer, or both, must often pay the franchiser a fee to assign the franchise. This transfer fee may be nominal, however, some franchisers require a new franchise fee. The seller and buyer should review the franchise agreement for the specific transfer rights, and obligations. Approval of the assignment should be incorporated within the purchase-and-sales agreement as a condition.

Many franchise agreements give the franchiser a right of first refusal to acquire the business on the same terms, in which case, waiver of the right of first refusal should be obtained, and of course, made another condition of the agreement. Franchisers who do not hold a right of first refusal may, nevertheless, attempt to take over the business by rejecting other potential buyers. The Federal Trade Commission monitors this coercive practice but with mixed results. Faced with such a franchiser, the buyer should abandon interest in the franchise system.

Valuing the franchised business can be more precise than with the independent business. Accounting records are usually detailed so the opportunity to conceal sales or distort profits is minimized by rigid franchiser controls. Also, the buyer can find out what new franchises, and existing franchises with similar sales, sell for.

The buyer of a franchised business must thoroughly investigate the franchiser. While few franchisees find fault with a McDonald's or a Holiday Inn, many franchise systems are shaky, which is why many franchised units are sold: the franchisee becomes disenchanted with the franchiser or senses the demise of the franchise system. He then attempts to recoup her investment by passing the problem onto the unwary buyer.

The buyer should investigate the franchiser by reviewing the franchiser's current disclosure statement which the franchiser must issue to all prospective franchisees—including transfers of existing franchised units. Many states have even stricter disclosure requirements. The disclosure statement's 20 points generally reveal the background and performance of the franchise. But seven points are particularly important:

1) Identification and experience of each of the franchiser's officers, director and key management personnel.

2) A description of lawsuits against the franchiser.

3) Prior bankruptcies of the franchiser and its officers and directors.

4) The number of existing franchisees, projected franchisees, terminated franchisees and those repurchased or not renewed by the franchiser.

5) A projection of franchisee profits and the number of franchisees achieving those profits.

6) The names and addresses of existing franchisees.

7) The franchisers financial statements. Disclosing these—and other items—is mandatory. However, no governmental agency verifies the accuracy of these disclosures so the buyer must investigate independently.

The nature of lawsuits against the franchiser is most important. While lawsuits against franchisers are common even in the best system, determine whether the litigation seems excessive or reveals serious problems within the franchise program.

> ⚠️ **CAUTION** The growth of the franchise system and the number of franchises that are renewed or terminated requires close study; the attrition rate should not exceed industry averages for the type franchise.

The buyer must also review the franchiser's financial statements that are part of its disclosure statement. Use caution: if the statements seem strong, if the income may come primarily from selling new franchises, not ongoing royalties. The latter builds franchise stability.

No investigation is complete without talking to other franchisees. They can best report the system's strengths and weaknesses—if you ask them the right questions:

- When and why did you buy the franchise?

- Why did you select this franchise?

- How effective was their training program?

- Did the franchiser fulfill its obligations in setting up the franchise?

- What do you buy from the franchiser? Are deliveries on time? Quality acceptable? Prices competitive?

- How adequate is the supervision?

- How effective is their training program?

- Do sales and profits compare favorably to those that were projected? Are they increasing?

- Has the franchiser fulfilled his obligations under the franchise agreement?

- What specific problems have you had with the franchiser? How have they been resolved?

- Are you satisfied with the franchise?

Poll a wide number of franchisees randomly. The International Franchise Association also encourages inquiries to suppliers, franchisees who have terminated affiliation, the Better Business Bureau and the regional office of the Federal Trade Commission.

If the franchise appears worthwhile from a business viewpoint, the franchise agreement should be reviewed next. The seller's franchise agreement may not apply to the buyer because franchisers continuously revise their agreement and they require the buyer-transferee to execute newer agreements which must be reviewed on these nine points:

1) *Franchise fees*

- ◆ What are the transfer fees?

- ◆ Is a new franchise fee charged for renewal?

- ◆ What are the ongoing royalties?

- ◆ How are royalties paid?

2) *Controls*

- ◆ Does the franchiser allow absentee ownership?

- ◆ Who sets the hours of operation?

- ◆ Who controls product selection?

- ◆ Are the sources of supply limited or controlled?

♦ Is pricing controlled?

♦ Is there an operations manual to follow?

3) *Support*

♦ Is training provided to the buyer?

♦ What are the details for training? Location? Cost?

♦ Will the buyer have start-up or takeover assistance?

♦ What continuing supervision does the franchiser provide?

♦ What legal or accounting services does the franchiser provide? Are they mandatory? What are the charges for these services?

♦ Is inventory control provided?

4) *Advertising and Promotion*

♦ What are the local/national advertising plans?

♦ Must the franchisee participate in promotional programs?

♦ Can the buyer do her own advertising? Is prior franchiser approval required?

♦ Is there a separate advertising charge?

5) *Non-competition*

♦ Is the territory exclusive?

♦ If non-exclusive, what competitive franchisees are planned for the geographic area?

♦ Can the franchiser own and operate its own units?

6) *Transfer*

- ◆ Can the franchise be sold, mortgaged or transferred?

- ◆ What are the transfer rights upon death?

- ◆ What are the restrictions on transfer?

- ◆ Does the franchiser have a repurchase option? A right of first refusal?

7) ***Duration and termination***

- ◆ What is the franchise period?

- ◆ Is the franchise renewable? On what terms?

- ◆ Is the new franchise fee payable upon renewal?

- ◆ What constitutes a default or breach? Is there a "cure" provision?

8) ***Financing***

- ◆ What restrictions impair the buyer's ability to finance the franchised acquisition?

- ◆ Does the franchiser offer financing assistance?

9) ***Guarantees***

- ◆ Are the franchisee's obligations under the franchise agreement personally guaranteed?

- ◆ What are the limitations and terms of the personal guarantee?

2) Buying the insolvent firm

The insolvent firm is one with more liabilities then assets. Many financially troubled businesses can not be marketed without first restructuring their debts.

Some sellers cannot reduce their debt, or do not want to make the effort. Their objectives may instead be to discharge personally guaranteed debts or tax obligations to which they have statutory liability. Sellers achieve this by either deferring the sale until cash flow can liquidate these debts, or by granting a security interest to those creditors who hold a personal guarantee. This gives these creditors payment priority over general creditors upon a sale or liquidation. The seller must keep the business out of bankruptcy for at least three months to prevent an avoidance of these security interests as preferences.

> **HINT**
> The seller who reduces the debts builds an equity in the business that puts money in his own pocket when it comes time to sell.

The owners of insolvent firms have other objectives. Some gladly exchange their troubled business for employment with the buyer. Others seek compensation on a non-compete agreement—that cannot be claimed by creditors. Or a seller may settle for a contingent payment, such as a personal bonus based on the future profitability or sales of the business.

Each objective has a common theme—to enrich the owner while creditors are forced to settle for pennies on the dollar. A seller who becomes a major beneficiary to this arrangement then cooperates so the buyer gets the business at the best possible price.

When acquiring the insolvent business directly from the seller, the buyer can proceed in three ways:

DEFINITION

1) The creditors may be asked to voluntarily compromise their aggregate debt to the purchase price or less. This must always be more than the liquidation value of the business. *Compositions*, or informal out-of-court debt consolidations, as they are sometimes called, can succeed when the business has only a few creditors and they all agree. Compositions are less successful when the company's creditors are too numerous or too unmanageable.

2) Creditors may be notified of the intended sale under the Bulk Sales Act. Since the proceeds will not fully pay the creditors, there must be strict conformity to the partial payment notice requirements under the Bulk Sales Act.

3) The seller may file for Chapter 11 reorganization and petition the court for permission to sell to the buyer. For the buyer, there is no safer bill of sale than one from the bankruptcy court. Similarly, the seller may make a general assignment for the benefit of creditors or petition for receivership, with the buyer positioned to then acquire the assets from the receiver or assignee.

These transfer strategies are not mutually exclusive. A seller, for example, may first attempt to compromise with creditors. Failing in that strategy, he may then attempt a direct sale with notice to creditors under the Bulk Sales Act. If that sale is blocked, the seller may then sell through the bankruptcy court or under an assignment for the benefit of creditors.

The choice of remedy is influenced by several factors. Larger firms ordinarily require a Chapter 11 to control the many conflicting creditor interests. The publicly traded buyer will want bankruptcy court approval because it requires more cautious dealings. Conversely, the small company may not find a Chapter 11 reorganization cost-justified, or the seller and buyer may simply prefer the faster more controlled sale under a Bulk Sales notice.

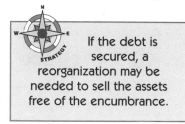

If the debt is secured, a reorganization may be needed to sell the assets free of the encumbrance.

Insolvency is a highly specialized area of law. Even experienced attorneys have little familiarity with its intricacies. Therefore, the buyer, seller, or both should obtain the guidance of an insolvency specialist who can chart the course to a smoother sale.

A buyer may want to buy a business in insolvency or liquidation. It may be a secured parties foreclosure sale, liquidation under assignment or receivership, or a bankruptcy trustee sale. In each instance, the business's owner has lost control over the disposition of the assets and plays no important role in the transaction.

The disadvantage to the buyer is that he may not gain the same information about the business as if she were dealing directly with the owner. The advantage is that the buyer would probably pay a far less than what the prior owner would have demanded.

The goal of the distressed business buyer is to acquire its assets for their appraised liquidation value. If the seller is a secured party, assignee, receiver or trustee, he can either liquidate at public auction or by private sale. If the private sale amount exceeds the appraised auction value,

note While the negotiating objectives under each type transaction are similar, the mechanics and legal considerations somewhat differ.

the sale is commercially reasonable and in the creditors' best interest. But these sellers usually still attempt to realize a higher price through competitive offers.

3) Purchase from secured party

A secured party may sell, lease or dispose of its collateral at either public or private commercially reasonable sale. The buyer acquires the secured assets free and clear of all subordinate lien holders and general creditors, given proper notice. The buyer under a secured party sale should also:

- Determine whether or not the security interest is duly perfected.

- Determine whether or not the collateral to be acquired is secured. The buyer must pay special attention to intangibles such as the name, goodwill, customer lists and trademarks which are often not secured and therefore cannot be sold by the secured party.

- Determine whether or not all statutory steps needed to legally take possession and sell the collateral have been followed.

- Review the appraisals to determine whether or not the private sale price exceeds the auction value and is therefore commercially reasonable.

- Determine if there are prior liens or encumbrances.

- Determine the debtors' rights to redeem the assets.

The buyer's counsel must review each of these even more carefully if the secured party does not tender a full warranty bill of sale, or if there is questionable recourse against the seller.

4) Purchase from an assignee or receiver

DEFINITION

Assignments and receiverships are similar. Both are non-bankruptcy methods of liquidation governed by state law. *Assignments* are voluntarily created by the debtor who appoints an assignee to liquidate the assets on behalf of the creditors. *Receivers* are usually court appointed on a creditor's petition. But, they have the same duties as the assignee—to liquidate the estate and pay creditors.

Both assignees and receivers accept the assets subject to their secured claims and prior encumbrances. Therefore, they can sell only the unencumbered interest in the assets, forcing the buyer to determine prior encumbrances against the business.

Buyer's counsel in each instance must review the state laws regulating sales by assignees and receivers. For an assignment, the buyer should review the assignment documents to determine that it is a proper assignment. Some states also require assignees and receivers to obtain judicial assent to any proposed sale. Creditors' notice and assents also may be required by state law or judicial order.

The assignee or receiver generally delivers only her title and does not give a full warranty bill of sale. This disadvantage requires extreme care by buyer's counsel.

5) Purchase from a bankruptcy trustee

Bankruptcy trustees routinely enter into private (nonauction) sales. Upon receipt of an acceptable offer, the trustee petitions the court for approval to sell. The court then orders the creditors notified of the intended sale and they may object or counteroffer.

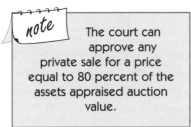

note The court can approve any private sale for a price equal to 80 percent of the assets appraised auction value.

Upon a court approved sale, the buyer obtains a trustees' bill of sale and certified court order confirming the sale. The court order essentially bars further claim against the assets sold. The buyer's counsel need only determine that the assets to be acquired were owned by the debtor and that the appropriate orders to sell have been obtained from the court.

This procedure closely parallels that followed by debtors-in-possession in Chapter 11. In Chapter 11 reorganization, the debtor also may sell under a liquidating plan of reorganization. Either practice is acceptable, but the one disadvantage with a liquidating plan is that it takes considerably longer to obtain court approval because the plan must first gain creditor approval.

6) Buying the service business

Buyers for the service business will find retaining the goodwill to be most important. Merely transferring a customer list has little value unless the customers continue to patronize the business.

Customer retention demands best faith efforts by both seller and buyer. While negative covenants—such as covenants not to compete—will help protect customer goodwill, affirmative steps are needed to maintain customers. This may be accomplished in several ways. Letters, personal introductions and joint announcements are reasonable expectations, or the seller may continue on with the business for a short interval after the acquisition until the buyer can obtain a foothold with his customers.

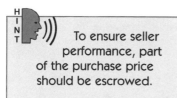

To ensure seller performance, part of the purchase price should be escrowed.

These affirmative obligations should not be a matter of verbal understanding; how the seller will cooperate must be incorporated within the agreement.

Many service businesses are sold under a price formula based on future sales so there is strong motivation for the seller to retain customers. The seller may otherwise be less inclined. Of course, in a formula price deal where the seller bears the risk, he will be concerned that the buyer will not maintain sales. The seller must carefully assess the buyer's prior performance and experience within the industry.

To retain goodwill, the buyer should consider asking the following questions:

◆ Will the buyer buy the business name? If the buyer plans to operate under another name, can the buyer use the seller's name in affiliation with her own?

◆ Will the buyer get the seller's telephone numbers and post office boxes?

◆ Will the buyer acquire the seller's pricing policies, operational data and other trade secrets?

◆ Will the non-compete agreement ensure non-solicitation of present and future accounts, as well as non-competition within the geographic market?

◆ Will the seller's key personnel agree to a similar non-compete agreement as a condition of employment?

◆ Will the seller agree to avoid damaging collection efforts on overdue accounts receivable?

◆ Does the agreement outline the respective seller/buyer obligations on warranty claims, merchandise returns and other obligations on sales that accrued prior to transfer?

7) Buying a partial business interest

The closely held corporation is usually sold in its entirety with the buyer gaining full ownership of the acquired business. This is true in both stock and asset transfers. With larger businesses, partial interest sales increase because the relationship between the existing and incoming owners is more financial than personal. These investments are often passive and do not involve day-to-day management between the parties.

When acquiring a business interest for investment purposes, the buyer must evaluate the company as a publicly-traded corporation. The difference is that if the closely-held corporation fails to perform satisfactorily, the buyer has no ready market for his interest. The prevailing objective then is to have the investment appreciate spectacularly and realize a gain when the company goes public. This is the investment goal of venture capitalists, SBICs and other institutional inventors. Smaller investors may only hope for an attractive return.

Regardless of objective, the passive investor invests in the management of the acquired company.

When the buyer plans on active management, she should determine if her objectives, methods and style are compatible with those of the remaining partners. Unfortunately, few buyers can really assess their compatibility before the acquisition. Only after the acquisition can operational or financial conflicts emerge.

Many buyers of a minority ownership interest become disillusioned. The buyers may have seen an occupational opportunity, only to be denied meaningful employment. Passive partners may see the business erode from chronic mismanagement. The obvious risks of a partial interest purchase must be counter-balanced by the clear possibility of spectacular gain.

HOT spot Control becomes a deciding factor when evaluating the acquisition. Whether the buyer anticipates a passive investment or management role, voting control provides management control should conflicts arise.

The degree of control is another consideration. Owning a 51 percent interest ensures managerial control, however greater ownership may be required to control major business decisions. The buyer must review the state-corporation laws and by-laws to determine the ownership needed to completely control the organization.

When larger corporations are the buyers, they usually insist on acquiring at least an 80-percent stock interest in what will become a subsidiary. Although a smaller ownership interest may ensure legal and functional control, the parent company must own at least 80 percent of its subsidiary's shares for tax consolidation purposes.

If the buyer does not buy a controlling interest, the buyer can nevertheless gain control:

- The buyer may receive an irrevocable proxy to vote some or all of the shares owned by the remaining partners.

- The corporation may issue a new class of non-voting shares that allows the buyer to control the voting class, while owning a smaller percentage of the total outstanding common stock.

- The bylaws may be amended to empower the buyer to appoint a select number of directors to the board.

- The business may contract to give the buyer certain managerial authorities and responsibilities.

DEFINITION

These possibilities are not mutually exclusive, but should be considered together. There are other safeguards. The buyer investing to become a working partner should require a long-term employment contract. The buyer and remaining partners also may option to sell and buy—or a *put and call*. This helps break a voting stalemate and at least

HOT spot All owners should become parties to the agreement and all steps needed to protect the relationship between the buyer and the residual owners should be undertaken simultaneous with the closing.

gives the buyer a graceful, orderly exit from the conflict-ridden business. The buyer alternatively may option to acquire the interests of the remaining owners. This objective is best when the buyer foresees a need for future investment beyond what the other owners can or will invest. These protections should not be negotiated after buying. They must be a condition of acquisition.

The seller, buyer and remaining owners must consider how to substitute the buyer for the seller on corporate obligations. The seller will want a release on those obligations to which she is a party—such as leases, notes and trade guarantees. The buyer will take her place as an obligor. When this is unacceptable to the creditor, the buyer should indemnify the buyer on these obligations. If the seller is to be released in exchange for the buyer's guarantee, the remaining owners, as guarantors to the obligations, must consider the buyer's financial strength for purposes of contribution upon default. The buyer will have equal concern of her partners' ability to pay their share of the business's liabilities.

8) Buying the partnership interest

The purchase and sale of a partnership interest compares closely to that of the partial interest with one important difference: the acquiring partner assumes full ownership of the business thus avoiding complex concerns over future control. Another difference is that the acquiring partner is familiar with the business.

note Partners buying the interests of their other partner(s) are common buy/sell deals. A significant number of small businesses are owned by two or more partners.

The term "partnership interest" does not necessarily imply a partnership form of organization. Except for the professional firm, few business organizations operate as true partnerships. Here the term more commonly applies to a corporate stock interest.

All too often, each partner will want to buy out the other. The issue then is who will buy and who will sell? Deadlocked, the partners often continue their infighting to the detriment of the business. Resolution comes only through eventual bankruptcy.

In this scenario, the partners must break their deadlock by forcing the sale from one to the other. The favored approach is to auction the business between the partners. They may stipulate the down payment and other terms of sale in advance and escrow the stock to ensure performance. The high bidder would obtain the business for what he sees as its value, while the selling partner receives more than what he considers the business to be worth. Neither party then has cause for complaint.

The one problem here is that one partner may have greater financial resources then the other and demand terms that cannot be matched by the opposing partner. Also, one or both partners may question the credit of the other under an installment buy-out. As with all seller financing, the only protection for a seller is the ability to reclaim an intact business upon a default.

The sale of a partnership interest usually follows the same procedures as a stock or redemption sale. Although the partners may sell the assets of a new entity created by the buying partner, the present business has contingent liabilities.

9) The gradual takeover

The gradual takeover is frequently used when employees gradually acquire ownership. It is also used to transfer businesses between generations. One example is a son who gradually assumes ownership control of a family-owned business. The gradual takeover essentially phases the transaction over time.

The gradual takeover is desirable when a seller plans to retire within several years and wants to slowly diminish his involvement in the business. The buyer's increasing ownership and responsibility supplements the seller's decreasing activities. It also assures the seller an agreed price for the business and the ability to remain active in the business while the purchase price is unpaid.

The gradual takeover attracts buyers for many of the same reasons. The buyer may be managerially unprepared for an immediate, total takeover and require the seller's transitional support. Also, the buyer may not be able to raise the down payment or financing for an immediate sale.

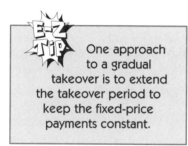
One approach to a gradual takeover is to extend the takeover period to keep the fixed-price payments constant.

Typically, the buyer acquires a set percentage of the stock each year—which the seller agrees to sell. This must be distinguished from a stock option plan in which the obligation to buy is discretionary, not mandatory, and seldom leads to more than a minority stockholder interest.

The gradual takeover, for example, may call for transfer of 10 percent of the stock for each of the first five years, with the remaining 50 percent transferred in the sixth year. The buyer may finance this final purchase through outside sources because she now has a paid-in equity, or the seller also may agree to finance the entire deal.

The price may be flexibly structured. The parties may set a fixed price to be paid over the term as the stock is transferred. The disadvantage is that the fixed price may not reflect the future value of the business. The buyer may then breach the agreement if the fixed price exceeds that value and the seller may be similarly tempted to default if the fixed price slides below.

The preferable approach is to reset the value of the stock to be acquired at each point using a formula to reflect the then current value of the business.

Even then there is a disadvantage, but one more easily solved: the price of the shares may increase beyond what the buyer can afford. The solution is to obligate the buyer to a stated amount of cash with further payments secured by a collateralized note.

Generally, the buyer finances purchase price payments through employment with the business. Profit sharing, bonuses, pension and similar plans often fund the acquisition. Since the seller controls the corporation, she also controls the compensation the buyer relies upon to buy. The seller may then intentionally force the buyer's breach.

Because the agreement contemplates a total takeover, both parties must guard against a breach by the other before full completion. The seller's shares should be escrowed to provide specific performance upon the buyer's tender of payment. Similarly, the buyer should be obligated to forfeit acquired shares upon default—and at a repurchase price appreciably below the acquisition price.

The gradual takeover is more than a long-term financial arrangement. As the buyer acquires a greater interest, the relationship between buyer and seller produces the same potential problems and conflicts as a partnership does. These conflicts may be more extreme as the managerial balance between the parties is not equal and stable but increasingly shifts from seller to buyer. Unlike ownership, it is impossible to contractually define management responsibility and authority. While the agreement should allow for the gradual shift of basic controls, the parties must design and develop the actual transition with the same mutual confidence that encouraged the transaction.

Closing the transaction

Chapter 12

Closing the transaction

Many factors influence the duties and responsibilities of the parties during the transitional stage between contract and closing.

One factor is the type of business being sold or acquired. A considerably different preclosing schedule is needed to sell a retail business, compared to a manufacturing or service business. The steps to safeguard the interests of the buyer and the seller in each type of transaction also vary.

The size and complexity of the company also alters the requirements, particularly when the company has many stockholders, involves regulatory requirements or complex financing. The nature of the transaction is another consideration. The parties will develop one schedule if the sale involves assets and another for a stock transfer or statutory merger.

Other factors include the time period between contract and closing, the volatility of the business during this transitional period and perhaps most importantly—the relationship and goodwill between the buyer and seller.

The pre-closing schedule

The buyer's counsel must prepare the work schedule as soon as possible in coordination with the seller's attorney, and the respective accountants.

The pre-closing work schedule has four important functions:

1) To help the parties and their counsel set a feasible closing date.

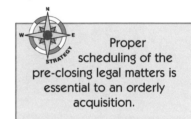

Proper scheduling of the pre-closing legal matters is essential to an orderly acquisition.

2) To establish a priority and timetable for each step necessary to close.

3) To serve as a checklist so important steps are not overlooked.

4) To divide responsibility for preparing documents and completing other pre-closing matters.

The parties must objectively assess the time it will require to complete the work and also the numerous contingencies that may delay the closing. A common problem is that the buyer and seller are usually anxious to close the transaction and may be insensitive to other matters competing for the professional's time. On the other hand, attorneys may needlessly delay, thus frustrating the client, the other parties to the transaction and perhaps jeopardizing the deal itself. So the attorneys must set a realistic timetable and explain to their respective clients the reasons for the timetable.

Inevitable problems delay a closing, therefore the agreement should provide for an outside closing date and allow extending when the delay is beyond the reasonable control of either party. Extending the closing should be acknowledged once it becomes apparent the closing cannot occur when scheduled.

Coordinating the closing documents

The work schedule starts with a complete itinerary of the documents required for closing. The attorneys should decide beforehand who will prepare each document, considering their respective work loads, skill, experience, the interests to be protected under each document, access to information needed for drafting, and what constitutes a fair division of work.

Presumably, the contract has been prepared and signed. As stated earlier, closing documents should be prepared with the contract and attached as exhibits to avoid later disputes concerning these documents, which usually include:

- bills of sale

- promissory notes (seller financing)

- security agreements

- financing statements

- assignment of contract rights

- seller's indemnification on liabilities

- lease or lease assignment

- transfer of telephone numbers

- Covenants Not To Compete

- seller's resolution authorizing sale

- buyer's resolution authorizing purchase

- reports on personal property searches

- waivers of tax claims

- transfers of certificates of title to motor vehicles

This list will invariably change. Many of these documents, commonly used for small business asset transfers, are model forms found in the forms section of this guide.

Satisfying contract conditions

The contract usually contains conditions precedent to the buyers closing, although a seller may impose his own conditions to concluding the sale. While conditions were discussed earlier, it is during the preclosing stage that each condition must be satisfied. Performance, for example, may be conditional upon the buyer obtaining:

- financing

- a satisfactory lease

- required licenses or permits

- a favorable tax ruling

- requisite stockholder consent

The parties should confirm, in writing, when each condition is satisfied. Conditions may not be satisfied within the set time. For example, a buyer may condition the agreement upon financing and encounter delays in obtaining a financing commitment. The seller must then decide whether or not to cancel or extend the contract.

If the seller is not satisfied with the buyer's progress in satisfying the conditions, the seller should terminate the contract by written notice. The seller may encourage further efforts by the buyer—that is, if the buyer can eventually satisfy the condition and the business remains unsold, then the contract may be restored. Until then, the seller can market the business. An alternative is to extend in return for a forfeitable deposit, if the condition still remains unsatisfied beyond the extension date.

> **CAUTION** Considering the numerous problems that can destroy a sale, neither party should enter into other commitments until the sale is actually concluded.

The seller should not change his position until all conditions to the agreement are fully satisfied. Frequently, for example, a seller will advise employees or customers of the pending sale, commit to relocation, or enter into new employment or a new business venture in reliance of a conditional contract. If the sale collapses, he can be hurt.

Beyond preparing the closing documents, the attorneys and accountants may be engaged in numerous activities to fulfill their own responsibilities and to assist their clients. These activities are considerable and include both legal and business items.

No pre-closing action checklist can fairly apply to every transaction. However, the checklist that follows exemplifies common items.

Seller's checklist

Actions by seller's counsel

- Update the corporate minute book.

- Obtain the seller's stock-transfer ledger and stock certificate book.

- Hold a stockholders' or directors' meeting to approve or confirm the sale.

- Obtain a certified copy of incorporation, certificate of good standing and state tax waivers.

- Obtain terminations of lease to be held in escrow pending the closing.

- Obtain discharge amounts on secured obligations.

- Obtain termination statements and discharges of encumbrances, to be escrowed pending closing.

- Obtain documents for the transfer of distributor and dealer agreements.

- Prepare the assignment of patents, trademarks and licenses.

- Terminate or assign the sellers pension plans, retirement plans, employment agreements, profit sharing agreements, and union contracts.

- Prepare affidavit of creditors' list Bulk Sales Act.

Actions by seller's account

- Assemble the financial information needed to prepare final tax returns.

- Prepare "cold-comfort letter" acknowledging no material adverse change in the financial condition.

- Update all financial records, ledgers and journals for delivery to buyer.

- Confirm the accuracy of seller's affidavit to creditors under the Bulk Sales Act.

- Reconcile the seller's bank accounts.

Actions by seller

- Prepare a list of creditors for affidavit under the Bulk Sales Act.

- Prepare a list of accounts receivable.

- Obtain copies of all insurance policies, agreements and debts to be assumed by buyer.

- Compile all other accounting, legal and business records to be delivered to the buyer.

- Reconcile accounts with all suppliers.

- Return goods for credit, where applicable.

- Remove personally owned items from the premises.

Buyer's checklist

Actions by buyer's counsel

- Verify the availability of the contemplated business name.

- Organize the buyer entity—corporation or partnership.

- Hold the necessary stockholders' or directors' meetings to approve purchase.

- Notify the seller's creditors under the Bulk Sales Act if applicable.

- Check liens or encumbrances against the property to be acquired.

- Prepare the banking resolutions for buyer entity.

- Conduct title search on any real estate to be acquired.

- Arrange for inventory tabulation.

- Obtain required insurance.

- Review and approve all buyer financing documents.

- Prepare new employment contracts, pension and profit sharing plans if the seller's plans are not assumed.

- Review all agreements, liabilities and debts to be assumed by buyer.

- Prepare and obtain executed lease or assignment of lease to be escrowed pending a closing.

- Obtain buyer's federal taxpayer identification number.

Avoiding last minute difficulties

Many additional requirements and problems can arise when preparing for the closing. No matter how thoroughly the preparation, loose ends and unexpected last minute difficulties arise. While they can be minimized with careful planning, they are best resolved with good faith and cooperative efforts between the parties.

> *note* Frequently, attorneys step in to resolve controversies between buyer and seller.

Not surprisingly, most transitional problems are business problems. Attorneys can usually overcome even the most serious legal developments, but the business transition may be more complicated. Experienced attorneys foresee many of these problems.

Four important steps that can help avoid these transitional problems:

1) *Close the transaction as quickly as possible.* While a reasonable time is needed to prepare for the closing, the greater the delay, the greater the chance for problems. Numerous changes can occur in

any business or in the parties attitude. Closings can and should occur within 30-60 days.

2) *The seller must maintain goodwill.* Problems occur when a seller shortens hours, raises prices, cuts credit or reduces the sales effort.

3) *Coordinate the transaction.* The buyer should be involved in every major decision likely to carry over beyond the closing.

4) *Employees, customers and suppliers should not be informed.* Some disclosure may be necessary during the business evaluation stage. However, widespread disclosure of a pending sale may create adverse rumors or reports to dampen the buyer's enthusiasm.

A balanced approach is for the seller and buyer to meet periodically to discuss and review key business developments and other items of transitional importance.

This raises the question of permissible buyer involvement in the business prior to the closing. Again, there is no one answer. However, most sellers prefer to keep the buyer from daily operations for fear it will disclose existing or potential problems and that the buyer will withdraw once exposed to these problems.

Closing the transfer

A detailed closing agenda and schedule of documents is absolutely essential for a smooth closing. Without preparation, the results are chaos and embarrassment. If the documents required for the closing are reviewed and approved by the respective counsel beforehand, the actual closing should be little more than a formal—and hopefully friendly—proceeding.

There is also a psychological factor. Whether a seller or a buyer, it is their moment of truth—the moment when they may develop second thoughts about the deal. Or the parties are hostile—usually the by-product of adversarial negotiations. Counsel who senses these problems should avoid the ritualistic closing and instead coordinate the closing between themselves with their clients absent.

The buyer's counsel is generally the closing's coordinator and master of ceremonies. Both counsel, however, must be sergeants-of-arms to keep the closing on a smooth track and prevent the parties from opening troublesome discussions. An orderly, well-run closing occurs with this properly planned agenda and with pre-approved documents.

The practical considerations when preparing for the closing start with the date, time and place. Although the contract will specify a closing date, invariably some other date must be selected. The most common closing date is the first day of the month because this makes the financial adjustments easier. Mondays may be advisable for the same reason. Or consider the payroll period. Arrange for a morning closing so there is time to complete the transaction on the same day should complications arise. It also provides ample time to record documents or obtain overlooked documents.

> **E-Z TIP** A well-drafted contract will outline the closing adjustments, but the parties must apportion payroll, vacation time, rent and occupancy costs, utilities and invoices for goods received after the inventory tabulation.

All required parties should attend, unless the documents were signed and executed earlier. For instance, the president of the company may appear without the corporate secretary, although the secretary must sign the corporate resolutions. A husband may leave a wife behind, although she is to be a guarantor on a note. Brokers, escrow agents, title companies, closers and other third parties to the transaction should also be present.

There are three ways to handle adjustments:

1) If the parties have a good relationship and can handle adjustments on their own, it may be left as a business matter beyond the scope of the closing.

2) Leave adjustments to the accountants for resolution immediately prior to the closing.

3) Hold a sum in escrow pending the resolution of disputed adjustments by an independent accountant appointed as arbitrator.

After the closing

The post-closing stage, like the pre-closing phase, is usually a flurry of legal, accounting and operational activity.

Regardless of the size, nature or complexity of the acquisition, the seller, buyer and their respective attorneys and accountants must come together to conclude the transaction. This is best handled with this eleven point post-closing agenda:

1) *Final title/lien check*. Buyer's counsel will check title and liens and encumbrances before closing, but there may be a title defect or recent attachment or lien. The closing documents and purchase price should be escrowed until a final post-closing search.

   • Updates the title for real estate acquired under the transaction.

   • Verifies there are no liens, attachments or security interests against the assets sold.

   • Verifies there are no security interests or liens against the buyer which would impair seller financing.

- Reviews court filings to verify there are no restraining orders or other impediments to the sale.

2) ***Document filing.*** The attorneys should prepare a specific recording agenda using the following checklist. The recording checklist includes:

  - financing statements to secure the seller's note

  - discharge of financing statements, security interests or encumbrances

  - deeds to real property included in the transaction

  - real estate mortgages due seller

  - discharges of prior mortgages and encumbrances on real estate conveyed to buyer

  - leases or notices of lease

  - assumed name certificates

  - assignments of patents, trademarks and copyrights with the U.S. Patent Office or state recording office

3) ***Financial adjustments.*** While most adjustments may be handled at closing, the post-closing adjustments may include:

  - inventory based on a post-closing evaluation

  - purchases made on seller's account, received by the buyer and not included in the inventory valuation

  - accounts receivable charge-backs on guaranteed but uncollected receivables

- rents, real estate taxes and other occupancy costs upon a final statement from landlord

- utility, fuel, oil and telephone charges upon presentation of final statements

- non-assumed liabilities arising subsequent to closing

- income received by buyer but due the seller

4) **Cancellations and terminations.** Unless assumed by the buyer, the seller should arrange for the cancellation and termination of:

- utility and telephone accounts

- insurance policies—and request a rebate on unused prepaid premiums

- contracts with service firms, including burglar alarm, security, maintenance and rubbish removal firms

- leases on loaned equipment and consigned personal property

- retainer agreements with accountants, attorneys, public relations firms, advertising agencies and other professionals

- leases and tenancies, including subleases

- guarantees by principals of the selling corporation in a stock transfer

- other executory contracts that are not assumed by the buyer

5) **Notification of transfer.** Public relations must be a part of every acquisition. Therefore, the buyer must be introduced to the various

business constituencies. The buyer and seller should prepare press releases, letters of introduction or other forms of notification to:

- employees

- customers—past and present

- distributors

- dealers

- sales representatives

- suppliers

- other professional advisors

- independent contractors

- depository banks

- lenders

6) *Transfers.* If the buyer assumes the seller's contracts, notification should be provided. Common transfers include the following:

- re-registration of motor vehicles

- insurance policies, including change of the insured and loss-payees

- cash on deposit to the buyer

- licenses, permits and registrations

- to the seller, retained corporate assets under a stock transfer

7) *Banking matters.* Under a stock sale, the buyer and seller must revoke existing signatories and issue new signature authorizations

to corporate accounts. Under an asset transfer, the seller must close all accounts and the buyer must open new accounts.

8) *Tax matters.* If the buyer is to operate under a new entity, he should obtain a federal taxpayer identification number, state, FICA and unemployment compensation registration. The seller should file final federal withholding tax, FICA, state withholding and sales tax, unemployment compensation returns, and final federal and state income tax returns.

9) *Insurance.* If the buyer is to assume the seller's insurance, the buyer should carefully review its coverage. Insurances should be obtained for:

- casualty

- public liability (at least in amounts required under the lease)

- workers' compensation

- business interruption

- motor vehicle

- product liability

- plate glass

- professional liability

- surety bonds

10) *Accounting matters.* Upon closing, the buyer's accountant must review the seller's accounting systems and financial controls and consider whether the buyer should adopt the same system, integrate new systems or design totally new accounting procedures.

Controls are essential for every business (payroll, accounts payable, receivable and general ledger), but the new acquisition requires more extensive financial planning and monitoring for the first year or two because sales costs and expenses are speculative and must continuously be adjusted. In particular, the

Because so many businesses are partially or totally computerized, incompatibility between buyer and seller systems may create transitional problems. If the seller is efficiently computerized, the buyer should bargain to take over the seller's system.

buyer will undertake substantial capital expenditures and have heavy financing commitments that threaten cash flow, and undergo significant change. The newly acquired business has great financial volatility.

The buyer's accountant must then prepare a:

- capital expenditure budget

- expense budget

- purchases budget

- a sales budget

- production cost analysis, if applicable

- a one year cash flow statement, projected monthly

11) *Corporate amendments.* There is a need for corporate amendments if the buyer acquires shares. Counsel for the buyer must then:

- Conduct the required corporate meetings to elect new directors and officers.

- File notice of change of officers and directors with the secretary of state where organized, and where it operates as a foreign corporation.

- Amend the corporate purpose to cover any planned change of business activity.

- Amend the by-laws to reflect the modifications required by the buyer.

- Update all prior minutes.

- Prepare minutes to ratify all acts required under the sale.

How to buy a business with no cash down

13

Chapter 13

How to buy a business with no cash down

You want to buy a business, but you don't have the money . . . do you give up? Not if you're smart! There are ways to make the impossible—possible. And the numbers prove it. So, armed with little more than hope, goals and a mountain of determination, you too can buck the odds, defy the rules and tweak the noses of conventional thinkers who stubbornly believe you really need money to make money.

HOT spot There are more than 14 million small businesses in the United States and about 20 percent are actively for sale.

Your down payment may be staring you right in the face and you still can't see it. It doesn't look like money, but it can be just as good if you have the imagination and know how to make it work for you.

You may see "cash-raising" possibilities never considered by the seller. After all, sellers can be short-sighted. They have been so close to their businesses for so long that they may not realize the potential gold mine locked up in their hidden assets. Don't you be blinded. The following seven tips will send you on your way to owning your own business with no cash down!

Strategy # 1: Let the seller's creditors finance the business

Assuming the seller's liabilities can go a long way toward covering the purchase price. For instance, if a company has $100,000 in assets but also has corresponding liabilities, what should you pay the seller? The answer is obvious—nothing. You can give the seller $1 for his or her interest in the company and assume all the assets and liabilities. Now you own the business with nothing invested. That's why troubled companies offer such interesting takeover targets like built-in financing.

Let's explore liability takeovers. First, you find that perfect boutique, then you analyze it from every direction until you're convinced you can make it successful. It's in obvious trouble. The seller says she's asking $75,000, but the books show it owes trade creditors $60,000. At best the seller can only clear $15,000 at the asking price. Once the seller admits this you have locked in $60,000 worth of financing. Later chapters in this book will show you how to get any other necessary moneys without dipping into your own cash.

Strategy #2: Let the suppliers finance the acquisition

Your business should be that proverbial money tree. Not only will it put money into your pocket year after year, it will also put money into the pockets of your suppliers. Those kind folks will benefit immensely from selling you merchandise inventory for that money-making business of yours. In fact, no matter how much money the business can earn for you, it may earn even more for your suppliers.

This brings us to a simple proposition. If your suppliers stand to profit from doing business with you, why not call upon them to advance some money that can put you into that business? You have plenty of persuasive arguments.

Imagine yourself negotiating for a $1 million-a-year market. The seller wants $100,000, but will finance 70% of the price, leaving you to find the down payment of $30,000.

With a little research you discover that the supermarket buys about 60 percent of its merchandise from one grocery wholesaler. Assuming the supermarket has a gross profit on sales of 25 percent, total annual purchases will be about $750,000 in purchases—$450,000 in merchandise—year after year.

Stick a price tag on that $450,000. What is it worth to the supplier? A little more research uncovers that grocery wholesalers take a 10 percent gross profit. With these numbers in mind you have a bargaining chip.

Strategy #3: Use the assets of the business to finance the down payment

You can often arrange to simultaneously sell some assets of the business when you buy the business. The sales proceeds from these assets can be used for a down payment.

Do a quick analysis. Does the company really need all the trucks it owns? Can you refinance the vehicles? Most businesses do not pledge vehicles as collateral for general business loans and therefore, even if the business has a mortgage against other assets, its vehicles are probably unpledged. In this situation, you can borrow against the vehicles and use the proceeds toward your down payment. You can do the same with equipment, real estate, and even tangible assets such as patents, trademarks and copyrights.

Strategy #4: Use cash flow from the business to cover the down payment

It's possible you can convince the seller to wait several weeks for his down payment, which can then come from the cash flow available to you after you take over the business.

This approach requires two steps. Although there are variations, the basic strategy always remains the same. First, determine the net cash flow generated by the business in the first several weeks by calculating the difference between cash receipts and what must be paid out. Next, structure the deal so the seller receives his down payment out of the cash flow.

> **E-Z TIP**
> Recruit a good accountant who can professionally guide you over the magic cash flow numbers quickly and accurately. It's not difficult to calculate what you can extract from the business.

Unfortunately, sellers will grow impatient to get their hands on the down payment you hope will appear from the cash flow. A sale can double or triple business and quickly raise your down payment.

Strategy #5: Have customers "frontload" your start-up or acquisition costs

Take a lesson from American Express. They have millions of cardholders and each pays a hefty membership fee to belong. Multiply this fee by the number of cardholders and you get an idea of what advance payments from customers can do to raise cash. And it can do the same for you. Just ask yourself that one question: which customers would pay you in advance?

This idea is not far-fetched. If you anticipate acquiring a business—and can offer customers a good incentive to "prepay"—you and the seller can create the down payment. For example, if you wanted to buy a health club, why not orchestrate a 25% discount advance membership fee? It can raise more than you need for a down payment.

Strategy #6: Turn a broker's commission into a down payment.

A broker's commission can be the answer to at least half your problem. The typical seller usually expects less than 30 percent of the sales price as a down payment. But bear in mind, that's only an expectation. If you study completed deals, you'll find the average down payment is less than 20 percent. The buyer usually raises the other 80 percent from a bank or through seller financing. Your job is to somehow reduce the 20 percent to zero.

Why should the broker loan you her commission? One good reason is that if she doesn't—the deal might collapse, leaving her without a commission. However, broker financing will not work if the broker thinks you can raise the down payment from other sources.

Strategy #7: Lease—don't buy— the business

Ownership isn't everything. You can often reap the same benefits from leasing a business as from buying it. And you may receive one added advantage: leasing can eliminate your down payment problem.

Many businesses lend themselves to leasing or purchasing on lease terms. Broadly speaking, they are service businesses whose limited assets are fixtures and equipment, such as gas stations, printing plants, car washes, auto-part stores, laundries and vending machine routes. These businesses can be easily leased because the seller doesn't have to worry about turning over inventory to you. Before the final agreement is reached, decide upon the method of transfer. The structure of the transaction involves important legal, financial and tax issues.

 For the smaller business, the sale can be accomplished by one of two methods. When the seller operates as a sole proprietorship or as a partnership, the sale must be handled as a sale of assets. Under a transfer of assets, the seller conveys to the buyer title to the assets acquired. The buyer typically sets up a new corporation to accept title, entering into new leases and contracts with employees, customer and suppliers.

The forms in this guide

NOTE: The forms in this publication have been reduced in size. To restore them to their correct size on a photocopier, increase the size to 122% .

About These Made E-Z Forms:
While the legal forms and documents in this product generally conform to the requirements of courts nationwide, certain courts may have additional requirements. Before completing and filing the forms in this product, check with the clerk of the court concerning these requirements.

AGREEMENT FOR SALE OF ASSETS

(Corporate Seller to Corporate Buyer)

AGREEMENT made and entered into by and between   ,
corporation with a usual place of business at   ,
                     ,   ("SELLER'), and   ,
another   corporation ("BUYER'), with a usual place of business at the same
location, all as their respective interests exist and are herein represented.

WHEREAS, SELLER operates a   at said aforementioned address and
is desirous of selling certain assets of the same to BUYER as a going business concern; and

WHEREAS, BUYER is desirous of purchasing said assets and continuing the operation of the
shoe business on terms as herein contained.

NOW, THEREFORE, it is for good and valuable consideration and in consideration of the
covenants, agreements, terms, and provisions as herein contained mutually agreed by and between the
parties as follows:

ARTICLE I: Sale of Assets

SELLER agrees to sell, and BUYER agrees to purchase and acquire all of the following assets,
chattels, and items as owned by, located on, and used in connection with the business of the SELLER
known as   .

a. All of the inventory, merchandise and goods for resale existing as of the date of closing.

b. All of the furniture, fixtures, equipment and supplies, furnishings, leasehold improvements
and without limiting the generality of the foregoing to include all office equipment, counters, shelves,
checkout units, cash registers, heating equipment, air conditioners, lighting fixtures, signs, display
units, decorative accessories and tools of the trade, accessories, appurtenances, provided and only to
the extent the same are located within the inside walls, ceiling and floor of the presently existing
location.

c. All of the goodwill of the SELLER, including such exclusive rights to the name
                     together with all policy manuals, price lists, supplier lists, customer
lists, secret formula, recipes or trade secrets to the extent they exist.

ARTICLE II: Assets to be Retained by Seller

SELLER shall retain all right, title and interest in and to the following items:

a. All cash on hand or on deposit.

b. All notes receivable, accounts receivable, prepaid expenses, utility deposits, tax rebates,
insurance claims, chooses in action; credits due from suppliers and other allowances.

c. Motor vehicles and automobiles.

d. Any equities in SELLER or any other incorporated or non-incorporated entity.

Specifically excluded also from any sale are any fixture, plumbing, wiring and/or equipment contained within the walls and/or attached to or upon the exterior walls or roof whether or not said fixtures, plumbing, wiring, and/or equipment passes through or is connected to the interior walls ceiling and/or floor of the presently existing ground-floor store or are fastened or connected to any item being sold to BUYER under this Agreement.

Specifically excluded also from any sale are any fixtures, plumbing, wiring and/or equipment contained within the walls and/or attached to or upon the exterior walls or roof whether or not said fixtures, plumbing wiring and/or equipment passes through or is connected to the interior walls ceiling and/or floor of the presently existing ground-floor store or are fastened or connected to any item being sold to BUYER under this Agreement.

ARTICLE III: Purchase Price

BUYER agrees to pay to SELLER, and SELLER agrees to accept as the full purchase price for all the singular the assets to be sold under Article I, supra; the total purchase price of
($) DOLLARS plus the cost value of the inventory at the time of closing as hereinafter defined and to be evaluated. At the time of closing, a physical inventory shall be conducted and tabulated by
("Tabulators"). The cost values shall be defined as retail price less   (%) percent. For illustration only, if an item has a retail price of ONE ($1) DOLLAR its cost value shall be   ($) CENTS. SELLER and BUYER shall mutually agree in the rejection or assignment of other partial values to any inventory for reason of questionable salability, marketability, retail value, or it being deteriorated, shopworn or otherwise not suitable for sale at full retail price; however, it is agreed that any item of inventory which can be returned to the distributor or manufacturer for full credit to BUYER shall not be rejected, but rather accepted at cost value, thereby giving BUYER the option of making any return. SELLER may retain title to any goods agreed upon as having no value. SELLER and BUYER each pay one-half (1/2) of the Tabulator's fee.

For illustration only, if the cost value of the inventory is determined to be
($) DOLLARS the total purchase price shall be
($) DOLLARS.

ARTICLE IV: Allocation of Purchase Price

The purchase price shall be allocated in the manner following:

$ Cost value as may be determined	For Article 1a assets
$	For Article 1b assets
$	For Article 1c assets
$	For Article 1d assets

ARTICLE V: Payment of Purchase Price

The purchase price as hereinabove to be determined in accordance with Article III, supra; shall be paid in the manner following:

deposit upon execution hereof by certified check to be held in escrow jointly by SELLER and BUYER.

at time of closing by certified check or bank check; provided that said amount shall be decreased pro rata if the total purchase price shall not equal $ any balance due thereafter, shall be paid timely ( ) days from date of closing.

ARTICLE VI: Sale Free and Clear

Seller agrees that it shall sell said assets free and clear of all liens, encumbrances, liabilities and claims of parties adverse thereto. SELLER agrees that it shall:

1. Waive all the conditions and requirements of the Bulk Sales Act; but SELLER shall complete and execute affidavit as annexed as Exhibit A.

2. At time of closing, SELLER shall provide BUYER with a tax waiver from the Department of Revenue, .

3. That any and all liens, encumbrances, security agreements, tax liens or attachments of record shall be fully discharges at time of closing.

4. SELLER shall provide BUYER with an indemnity agreement as annexed as Exhibit B, indemnifying BUYER from any asserted claims against assets sold to BUYER.

ARTICLE VII: Seller's Warranties

The SELLER warrants and represents to BUYER with knowledge the BUYER shall rely on same to enter into this transaction, each and all of the foregoing:

a. That the SELLER owns all and singular the assets being sold hereunder, and has full marketable title to same excepting only for items set forth on Exhibit C, "non-owned assets."

b. That the SELLER has full right and authority to enter into this agreement and right to perform and sell hereunder.

c. That there are no known eminent domain or condemnation proceedings affecting the ground store area containing the shoe business or any of its common areas.

d. That at the time of the sale, all fixtures, equipment, air conditioners, heating equipment and other apparatus shall be in good working order at the time of passing except those items which, upon the date of this Agreement, not functioning. Acceptance of the bill of sale by BUYER shall be conclusive evidence of satisfaction of this warranty. The parties agree that the amount of consideration paid for the above fixtures, equipment, air conditioners, heating equipment and other apparatus is based upon the fact that these items above being bought and sold "as is" and SELLER disclaims any warranty of merchantability for periods beyond the closing, and BUYER accepts the same "as is" and hereby waives forever any rights he may have had otherwise.

e. That there are no known governmental or administrative proceedings against SELLER, including but not limited to, the Board of Health or Building Inspector, which have arisen due to, or in connection with, its conduct of its business.

ARTICLE VIII: Covenant not to Compete

SELLER agrees and covenants that it shall not compete with the supermarket business being transferred herein; pursuant to the terms of the covenant not to compete agreement as annexed as Exhibit D.

ARTICLE IX: Seller's Obligation Pending Closing

SELLER agrees, warrants and covenants that during the pendency of this agreement, that:

1. SELLER shall maintain customary store hours.

2. SELLER shall maintain its customary and usual pricing and promotional programs.

3.SELLER shall maintain adequate stock necessary to maintain the goodwill of the business

4. SELLER shall not conduct any liquidation or so-called close-out sales.

5. SELLER shall maintain the current employees for the benefit of BUYER; however, nothing herein shall prevent a discharge for cause or require BUYER to employ any present employees.

Acceptance of the bill of sale shall be conclusive evidence of satisfaction of this Article IX. In the event of any asserted breach, BUYER shall give SELLER written notice thereto and SELLER shall cure within three (3) days thereafter. In the event SELLER shall not so cure, then BUYER shall have the option to terminate this Agreement without further recourse to either party thereto.

ARTICLE X: Casualty

It is further provided that if there is any casualty, destruction, or loss to the assets described in Article 1b in an amount equal to or in excess of ten (10%) percent of the total value; then in such instance this Agreement may be terminated at the election of BUYER, unless said assets or premises shall, before the date of closing be restored or replaced to their former condition.

ARTICLE XI: Conditions-Precedent-Concurrent-and-Subsequent

This agreement and all of BUYER'S obligations hereunder shall be fully conditional upon the occurrence of the following:

BUYER obtaining a lease for the present premises of SELLER, together with certain land purchase options as included therein ("Lease") and as annexed hereto as Exhibit E. It is expressly agreed and understood that this Agreement and the Lease shall be mutually dependent; and BUYER shall not be obligated to perform under the Agreement without benefit of said Lease and reciprocally BUYER shall have no rights under said Lease unless the sale is concluded under this Agreement. The purchase options are attached as Exhibits F, G and H.

ARTICLE XII: Brokers

The parties warrant and represent to each other that there are no brokers to this transaction and none entitled to commission.

ARTICLE XIII: Adjustments

The parties agree that at the time of closing they shall prorate and adjust for allocable and other expenses subject to adjustment in the manner following:

1. Merchandise ordered by SELLER prior to closing but received by BUYER subsequent to closing and therefore not tabulated in the inventory shall either be (a) paid for by BUYER or (b) rejected by BUYER and returned to shipper for credit to SELLER. BUYER agrees to indemnify and hold harmless SELLER for BUYER'S failure to comply with this provision. This paragraph shall survive the closing date.

2. There shall be no adjustment for yellow page advertising, electric, telephone or gas as buyer shall simultaneously with closing establish its own accounts.

3. There shall be no adjustment for insurance premiums as BUYER shall obtain its own insurance.

4. Payroll (excepting for accrued wages, benefits) shall be adjusted. There shall be an adjustment for fuel oil, rent, burglar alarm rentals and service contracts (provided that nothing herein shall obligate BUYER to assume any executory contracts of SELLER).

ARTICLE XIV: Miscellaneous

1. All Exhibits are hereby incorporated by reference.

2. This constitutes the entire agreement and there are no other terms, conditions, warranties, representations or inducements except as are expressly set forth herein.

3. Headings are for convenience only and are not an integral part of this Agreement.

4. The parties shall do, undertake, execute and perform all acts and documents reasonably required to carry out the tenor and provisions of this Agreement.

ARTICLE XV: Closing

The closing shall be on   ,   (year) at   at office of SELLER.

Time is of the essence.

Signed under seal this   day of   ,   (year).

BY: _____

BY: _____

PRINCIPALS:

Date: _____   _____
                                                Principal

Date: _____   _____
                                                Principal

257

AGREEMENT:
(Sale of Entire Corporation Under a Stock Redemption)

AGREEMENT made and entered into by and between

of   ,   (hereinafter "SELLER");

                            an   corporation with a usual place of business at

                                        ,   ,   (hereinafter

"CORPORATION");   , another

corporation at   ,   ,

(hereinafter "BUYER");   (hereinafter "   "),

                            ,   ; all as their respective interests exist and are herein

represented.

WHEREAS, SELLER is the owner of all the issued and outstanding shares of stock of the CORPORATION and is desirous of selling and transferring all of shares to the CORPORATION under a redemption, all as contained hereunder, and

WHEREAS, the CORPORATION is desirous of purchasing and acquiring said shares, redeeming same, and retiring said shares as non-voting treasury stock, and otherwise fulfilling the terms and conditions as herein contained, and

WHEREAS, the CORPORATION is desirous of issuing new shares to the BUYER and the BUYER is desirous of acquiring said shares from the CORPORATION, with the intent that upon consummation of this agreement, the BUYER shall be the sole stockholder of all the issued and outstanding shares of stock of the CORPORATION, and

WHEREAS, as an inducement for the SELLER to enter into this agreement,
and   as the principals of BUYER agree to guarantee certain obligations of the CORPORATION hereunder.

WITNESSETH: That for one dollar and other good and valuable consideration of the agreements, conditions, terms, provisions, covenants, representations and inducements as herein contained, it is mutually and reciprocally agreed by and between the parties as follows:

ARTICLE I: Sale of Shares by Seller

SELLER hereby agrees to sell and transfer, and the CORPORATION agrees to purchase, acquire and redeem, all the shares of stock in and to the CORPORATION as owned and held by SELLER, said shares being further described as shares of common stock, evidenced by stock certificate number 2, and being further referred to hereinafter as SELLER'S shares.

ARTICLE II: Seller's Representations as to Seller's Shares

The SELLER expressly warrants and represents to the BUYER each of the following:

1. That the described SELLER'S shares represents all of the issued and outstanding shares of the CORPORATION, of all classes inclusive, and there are no outstanding subscriptions to sell further shares other than as shall be entered into by BUYER pursuant to this agreement.

2. That the SELLER has good and marketable title to the SELLER'S shares.

3. That said SELLER'S shares are fully paid and non-assessable.

4. That said SELLER'S shares are free from lien, encumbrance, pledge, sequestration and shall be transferred free of any adverse claim thereto.

5. That there are no outstanding proxies, assignment of rights or other form of stock power transfer arising from SELLER'S shares.

6. That all required waiver of restrictions on transfer of SELLER'S shares have been obtained.

7. That upon transfer, the CORPORATION shall have good and marketable title to all the presently outstanding shares.

ARTICLE III: Purchase Price

The CORPORATION agrees to pay to the SELLER for the purchase and redemption of the SELLER'S shares, a price equal to the cost value of the inventory plus $; and to be subtracted from said combined sum shall be all existing liabilities of the CORPORATION at the time of transfer, all as further defined below. In addition to the purchase price, as so defined, the CORPORATION shall further transfer to the SELLER certain assets of the CORPORATION as assets of the CORPORATION as set forth in Article VI, infra.

For purposes of determining the cost value of the inventory for the parties shall cause a physical tabulation of all inventory for resale owned by the CORPORATION to be conducted by   ("Tabulators"), immediately prior to sale hereunder. The Tabulators shall value the inventory at cost, inclusive of customarily prevailing trade, cash or quantity discounts. The Tabulators shall reject from tabulation and inventory which in their judgment is unmerchantable or unsalable, which may be removed by SELLER. Items of questionable value may have partial values assigned. The determination by the Tabulators of the cost value shall be binding upon the parties and deemed conclusive. The SELLER and BUYER shall each pay one-half of the Tabulators fee.

The term "existing liabilities" as used herein shall mean and include all debts, obligations and liabilities of the CORPORATION existing or accrued at time of transfer hereunder, including but not limited to: Accounts payable, expenses payable, notes payable, taxes accrued to date, accrued wages, rents, loans due any party, and obligations of every nature and description, whether secured or unsecured, disputed or undisputed, known or unknown, liquidated or unliquidated, presently due or due at a future time, contingent or non-contingent and notwithstanding whether the CORPORATION'S liability is primary or secondary. Exempted from liabilities are contingent claims, known or unknown, for which there is adequate insurance coverage, and further exempted are all interest charges, service fees, penalties, or other like assessments for late payment accrued from date of transfer. The BUYER shall prepare a schedule of liabilities as above defined, and annex same at time of transfer as Exhibit A.

ARTICLE IV: Recourse for Unlisted Liabilities

SELLER represents and warrants to the BUYER that the only debts, obligations and liabilities of the CORPORATION at time of transfer shall be those scheduled and contained on Exhibit A. In the event any debt, liability or obligation not scheduled thereinafter arise to be asserted, or asserted by any creditor or claimant in excess of that listed, then in such instance.

1. The CORPORATION and BUYER shall have full rights to indemnify as against the SELLER pursuant to indemnity agreement as set forth as Exhibit B ("indemnity agreement").

2. In the event SELLER shall fail to promptly and fully indemnify under said indemnity agreement, then in such instance, the CORPORATION may as a further cumulative remedy pay or otherwise satisfy or discharge said unscheduled liability and deduct said expended payment from the next due installment(s) due under the promissory note due SELLER as further described in Article, infra.

ARTICLE V: Payment of Purchase Price

The purchase price as shall be determined in accordance with Article IV, supra, shall be paid in the manner following; at time of sale:

$ _____ By cash or certified check, funded by a payment to the CORPORATION of the subscription price for a new stock issue of corporate shares to BUYER pursuant to stock subscription to be entered into by BUYER under Article 8.

$ _____ Evidence by a promissory note for said balance amount payable in 72 monthly installments with interest thereon at 10 percent per annum on the unpaid balance, all as set forth in Exhibit C, ("note").

Said not shall be further secured by a senior security interest on all assets of the CORPORATION, all as set forth in Exhibit D, to be fully perfected in accordance with the Uniform Commercial Code.

Said note shall be further secured by a certain guarantee of BUYER,   and   , jointly and severally pursuant to guarantee annexed as Exhibit E ("guaranty").

Said guarantee and note shall be further secured by a pledge to SELLER of all the issued and outstanding shares of the CORPORATION pursuant to pledge agreement annexed as Exhibit F.

ARTICLE VI: Additional Transfers to Sellers

As additional compensation and payment to the SELLER, for the purchase and redemption of the SELLER'S shares, the CORPORATION shall transfer and convey to SELLER at time of closing:

1. All cash on hand and on account.

2. All accounts receivable including Medicaid receivables accrued to date; to be transferred without recourse.

3.   , sold subject to a lien on said vehicle to be paid and discharged by SELLER.

In accordance with the foregoing, the CORPORATION shall execute and deliver to SELLER a Bill of Sale as annexed as Exhibit G.

ARTICLE VII: Redemption by Corporation

The CORPORATION agrees and acknowledges that upon sale and transfer to it of all of SELLER'S shares as hereinbefore contained, it shall thereupon cause said shares to be held as nonvoting treasury stock.

ARTICLE VIII: New Stock Issue to Buyer

Simultaneous with the sale and redemption to the CORPORATION of the SELLER'S shares, the BUYER shall acquire 10 shares of the CORPORATION, under a new stock issue, all pursuant to a stock subscription agreement annexed as Exhibit H, and the CORPORATION shall accept said subscription, and upon payment of the full subscription price issue said shares to the BUYER, the intent being that upon issue, the BUYER shall thereupon own all the issued and outstanding shares of the CORPORATION.

ARTICLE IX: Additional Warranties of Seller

As an inducement for BUYER to enter into this agreement, and in acknowledgement that BUYER shall rely upon same, the SELLER expressly makes the following warranties and representations to the BUYER relative to the CORPORATION and its affairs:

1. That the CORPORATION is in good standing as an   corporation

2. That all tax returns or filings due any taxing authorities have been duly tiled and paid.

3. That the CORPORATION has good and marketable title to all assets, chattels or properties on its premises or used in connection with its business excepting only for scheduled non-owned items listed on Exhibit 1.

4. That the present lease held by the CORPORATION is set forth as Exhibit J, and that said lease is without modification or change, is in full force and effect, in good standing, and there are no known breaches thereto by the CORPORATION, and there are no known proceedings to evict, terminate said lease, or otherwise curtail or impair the tenancy or the CORPORATION'S rights thereunder.

5. That the only security interest, conditional sale, lease- option agreement, lien or encumbrance against any asset of the CORPORATION are scheduled on Exhibit K, and said security interest (or other UCC Article 9 transaction) remains in force without default, and there are no known proceedings to foreclose, terminate, replevy or repossess any asset so secured.

6. That there are no known lawsuits pending against the CORPORATION.

7. That there are no known audits pending against the CORPORATION by any governmental body, including any taxing authority or Medicaid agency.

8. That the CORPORATION is not bound on any executory contract other than contracts terminable at will, without penalty or breach (excepting for lease or scheduled security agreements) other than those listed on Exhibit L.

9. That to the SELLER'S best knowledge and reasonable belief, the existing liabilities scheduled on Exhibit A are materially and substantially accurate and all inclusive.

ARTICLE X: Covenant not to Compete

The SELLER further agrees to execute and deliver to the CORPORATION a covenant not to compete as set forth as Exhibit M. It is understood that the consideration for this covenant shall be $1.00 and not the purchase price for the redeemed shares, in whole or in part.

ARTICLE XI: Resignations

The SELLER shall at time of transfer provide BUYER with the resignations of all officers and directors of the CORPORATION as set forth on Exhibit M, and thereafter BUYER as sole stockholder of the CORPORATION shall install new officers and directors and promptly cause notice of change of officers and directors to be filed with the Secretary of State.

ARTICLE XII: Adjustments

The parties agree to adjust and pro rate certain allocable expenses and other apportionable charges including:

1. Wages and vacation pay

2. Rent

3. Utility charges

4. Prepaid expenses

ARTICLE XIII: Transitional

Obligations The parties agree to do, undertake and perform all acts reasonably required or incidental to ensure an orderly transition of ownership control, which shall include but not necessarily be limited to:

1. The SELLER shall deliver to BUYER all books, records, documents, invoices, tax returns, insurance policies, corporate records and books and other written properties of the CORPORATION, and shall to the extent reasonably required familiarize BUYER with the operation of the business.

2. The parties further agree to execute and deliver any further documents reasonably required or incidental to fulfill and perform the tenor of this agreement.

ARTICLE XIV: Brokers

The parties acknowledge that   ,   ,
                    ,   is the broker to this transaction and is due a brokers fee of $ payable by the SELLER at time of closing.

ARTICLE XV: Releases

SELLER and CORPORATION agree to release and discharge one and the other from any and all liabilities an obligations between them (excepting for those obligations created by this agreement intended to survive), pursuant to release annexed as Exhibit N.

ARTICLE XVI: Miscellaneous

1 All exhibits are herein incorporated by specific reference.

2. This constitutes the entire agreement and there are no other terms, conditions, warranties representations or inducements made or relied upon, other than as expressly contained.

3. This agreement shall be binding upon and inure to the benefit of the parties, their successors, assigns, and personal representatives.

4. This agreement is executed with copies, and executed copies shall have the full force of executed originals.

ARTICLE XVII: Closing

The date for closing shall be _____ , _____ (year) at _____ , at the office of _____ , _____ , _____ .

Signed under seal this _____ day of _____ , _____ (year).

_____
Signature for Seller

_____
Signature for Buyer

State of _____ }
County of _____
On _____ before me, _____ , appeared _____
personally known to me (or proved to me on the basis of satisfactory evidence) to be the person(s) whose name(s) is/are subscribed to the within instrument and acknowledged to me that he/she/they executed the same in his/her/their authorized capacity(ies), and that by his/her/their signature(s) on the instrument the person(s), or the entity upon behalf of which the person(s) acted, executed the instrument.
WITNESS my hand and official seal.

_____
Signature of Notary

Affiant _____ Known _____ Produced ID
Type of ID _____
(Seal)

PROMISSORY NOTE

Principal amount $ Date:

FOR VALUE RECEIVED, the undersigned hereby jointly and severally promise to pay to the order of   the sum of
Dollars ($), together with interest thereon at the rate of   % per annum on the unpaid balance. Said sum shall be paid in the manner following:

All payments shall be first applied to interest and the balance to principal. This note may be prepaid, at any time, in whole or in part, without penalty.

This note shall at the option of any holder thereof be immediately due and payable upon the occurrence of any of the following: 1) Failure to make any payment due hereunder within days of its due date. 2) Breach of any condition of any security interest, mortgage, loan agreement, pledge agreement or guarantee granted as collateral security for this note. 3) Breach of any condition of any loan agreement, security agreement or mortgage, if any, having a priority over any loan agreement, security agreement or mortgage on collateral granted, in whole or in part, as collateral security for this note. 4) Upon the death, incapacity, dissolution or liquidation of any of the undersigned, or any endorser, guarantor to surety hereto. 5) Upon the filing by any of the undersigned of an assignment for the benefit of creditors, bankruptcy or other form of insolvency, or by suffering an involuntary petition in bankruptcy or receivership not vacated within thirty (30) days.

In the event this note shall be in default and placed for collection, then the undersigned agree to pay all reasonable attorney fees and costs of collection. Payments not made within five (5) days of due date shall be subject to a late charge of   % of said payment. All payments hereunder shall be made to such address as may from time to time be designated by any holder.

The undersigned and all other parties to this note, whether as endorsers, guarantors or sureties, agree to remain fully bound until this note shall be fully paid and waive demand, presentment and protest and all notices hereto and further agree to remain bound, notwithstanding any extension, modification, waiver, or other indulgence or discharge or release of any obligor hereunder or exchange, substitution, or release of any collateral granted as security for this note. No modification or indulgence by any holder hereof shall be binding unless in writing; and any indulgence on any one occasion shall not be an indulgence for any other or future occasion. Any modification or change in terms, hereunder granted by any holder hereof, shall be valid and binding upon each of the undersigned, notwithstanding the acknowledgement of any of the undersigned, and each of the undersigned does hereby irrevocably grant to each of the others a power of attorney to enter into any such modification on their behalf. The rights of any holder hereof shall be cumulative and not necessarily successive. This note shall take effect as a sealed instrument and shall be construed, governed and enforced in accordance with the laws of the State of

.

Witnessed:

_____   _____
Witness   Borrower

_____   _____
Witness   Borrower

GUARANTY

We the undersigned jointly and severally guaranty the prompt and punctual payment of all moneys due under the aforesaid note and agree to remain bound until fully paid.

In the presence of:

_____   _____
Witness   Guarantor

_____   _____
Witness   Guarantor

GUARANTY

FOR GOOD CONSIDERATION, and as an inducement for _____ (Creditor), from time to time extend credit to _____ (Customer), it is hereby agreed that the undersigned does hereby guaranty to Creditor the prompt, punctual and full payment of all monies now or hereinafter due Creditor from Customer.

Until termination, this guaranty is unlimited as to amount or duration and shall remain in full force and effect notwithstanding any extension, compromise, adjustment, forbearance, waiver, release or discharge of any party obligor or guarantor, or release in whole or in part of any security granted for said indebtedness or compromise or adjustment thereto, and the undersigned waives all notices thereto.

The obligations of the undersigned shall at the election of Creditor be primary and not necessarily secondary and Creditor shall not be required to exhaust its remedies as against Customer prior to enforcing its rights under this guaranty against the undersigned.

The guaranty hereunder shall be unconditional and absolute and the undersigned waive all rights of subrogation and set-off until all sums due under this guaranty are fully paid. The undersigned further waives all suretyship defenses or defenses in the nature thereof, generally.

In the event payments due under this guaranty are not punctually paid upon demand, then the undersigned shall pay all reasonable costs and attorney's fees necessary for collection, and enforcement of this guaranty.

If there are two or more guarantors to this guaranty, the obligations shall be joint and several and binding upon and inure to the benefit of the parties, their successors, assigns and personal representatives.

This guaranty may be terminated by any guarantor upon fifteen (15) days written notice of termination, mailed certified mail, return receipt requested to the Creditor. Such termination shall extend only to credit extended beyond said fifteen (15) day period and not to prior extended credit, or goods in transit received by Customer beyond said date, or for special orders placed prior to said date notwithstanding date of delivery. Termination of this guaranty by any guarantor shall not impair the continuing guaranty of any remaining guarantors of said termination.

Each of the undersigned warrants and represents it has full authority to enter into this guaranty.

This guaranty shall be binding upon and inure to the benefit of the parties, their successors, assigns and personal representatives.

This guaranty shall be construed and enforced under the laws of the state of

.

Signed this   day of   ,   (year).

In the presence of:

_____   _____
Witness   Guarantor

_____   _____
Witness   Guarantor

SECURITY AGREEMENT

AGREEMENT made this   day of   ,   (year) between
("Debtor") and   ("Secured Party").

1. *Security Interest.* Debtor grants to Secured Party a security interest ("Security Interest") in all personal property and fixtures including inventory, equipment, and other goods, documents, instruments, general intangibles, chattel papers, accounts, and contract rights (as such terms are defined by the Uniform Commercial Code as in effect in   from time to time [the "Uniform Commercial Code"] in which Debtor now has or hereafter acquires any right and the proceeds therefrom ("Collateral"). The Security Interest shall secure the payment and performance of Debtor's promissory note dated the date hereof in the principal amount of
($) ("Note"), a certain Loan Agreement dated the date hereof by and between Debtor and Secured Party and the payment and performance of all other liabilities and obligations of Debtor to secured Party of every kind and description, direct or indirect, absolute or contingent, due or to become due, now existing or hereafter arising (collectively with the Note called the "Obligation").

2. *Financing Statements and Other Action.* Debtor agrees to do all acts which Secured Party deems necessary or desirable to protect the Security Interest or to otherwise carry out the provisions of this Agreement, including but not limited to, the execution of financing, continuation, amendment and termination statements and similar instruments and the procurement of waivers and disclaimers of interest in the Collateral by the owners of any real estate on which the Collateral is located. Debtor appoints Secured party as Debtor's attorney irrevocable to do all acts which Debtor may be required to do under this Agreement.

3. *Debtor's Place of Business.* Debtor warrants that:

   (a) Debtor's principal place of business is located at   ,

            ,   ;

   (b) Debtor has no other place of business;

   (c) The records concerning Debtor's accounts and contract rights are located at its principal place of business;

   (d) The record owners of the real estate on which any of the Collateral is located and their addresses are:

Debtor covenants to notify Secured Party of the addition or discontinuance of any place of business or any change in the information contained in this paragraph 3.

4. *Location of Collateral.* Debtor warrants and covenants that all of the Collateral shall be located:

(a) at Debtor's principal place of business specified in paragraph 3(a) of this Agreement;

(b) in a safe deposit box in the Debtor's name at   .

(c) in bank accounts in Debtor's name at   .

(d) in such other locations as are set forth on Exhibit A hereto.

None of the Collateral shall be removed from the locations specified in this paragraph other than in the ordinary course of business.

5. *Encumbrances.* Debtor warrants that Debtor has title to the Collateral and that there are no sums owed or claims, liens, security interest or other encumbrances against the Collateral. Debtor covenants to notify Secured Party or any claim, lien, security interest or other encumbrance made against the Collateral and shall defend the Collateral against any claim, lien, security interest or other encumbrance adverse to Secured Party.

6. *Maintenance of Collateral.* Debtor shall preserve the Collateral for the benefit of Secured Party. Without limiting the generality of the foregoing, Debtor shall:

(a) make all repairs, replacements, additions and improvements necessary to maintain any equipment in good working order and condition;

(b) maintain an inventory sufficient to meet the needs of its business;

(c) preserve all beneficial contrast rights; (d) take commercially reasonable steps to collect all accounts; and

(e) pay all taxes, assessments, or other charges on the Collateral when due.

Debtor shall not sell, lease or otherwise dispose of any item of the Collateral except in the ordinary course of business and shall not use the Collateral in violation of any law.

7. *Maintenance of Records.* Debtor covenants to keep accurate and complete records listing and describing the Collateral. When requested by Secured Party, Debtor shall give Secured Party a certificate on a form to be supplied by Secured Party listing and describing the Collateral and setting forth the total value of the inventory, the amounts of the accounts and the face value of any instruments. Secured Party shall have the right at any time to inspect the Collateral and to audit and make copies of any records or other writings which relate to the Collateral or the general financial condition of Debtor. Secured Party may remove such records and writings for the purpose of having copies made thereof.

8. *Collection of Accounts.* Secured Party may communicate with account debtors in order to verify the existence, amount and terms of any accounts or contract rights. Secured Party may at any time notify account debtors of the Security Interest and require that payments on accounts and returns of goods be made directly to Secured Party. When requested by Secured Party, Debtor shall notify account debtors and indicate on all billings that payments and returns are to be made directly to Secured Party. Secured party shall have full power to collect, compromise, endorse, sell or otherwise deal with the accounts or proceeds thereof and to perform the terms of any contract in order to create accounts in Secured Party's name or in the name of Debtor.

If any of Debtor's accounts or contract rights arise out of contracts with a governmental body subject to the Federal Assignment of Claims Act or a similar statute, Debtor shall notify Secured party thereof in writing and execute any instruments and take any action required by Secured Party to ensure that all monies due and to become due under such contract shall be assigned to Secured Party.

This Agreement may but need not be supplemented by separate assignments of accounts and contract rights and if such assignments are given the rights and security interests given thereby shall be in addition to and not in limitation of the rights and Security Interest given by this Agreement.

9. *Insurance.* Debtor shall maintain insurance covering the Collateral against such risks, with such insurers, in such form, and in such amounts as shall from time to time be reasonably required by Secured Party; provided, however, that the amount of said insurance coverage shall at all times equal or exceed the fair market value of the Collateral and in no event be less than $.
All insurance policies shall be written so as to be payable in the event of loss to Secured party and shall provide for ten (10) days' written notice to Secured Party of cancellation or modification. At the request of Secured Party, all insurance policies shall be furnished to and held by Secured Party. Debtor hereby assigns to Secured Party return premiums, dividends and other amounts which may be or become due upon cancellation of any such policies for any reason whatsoever and directs the insurers to pay Secured Party any sums do due. Secured Party is hereby appointed as attorney irrevocable to collect return premiums, dividends and other amounts due on any insurance policy and the proceeds

of such insurance, to settle any claims with the insurers in the event of loss or damage, to endorse settlement drafts and in the event of a default under this Agreement to cancel, assign or surrender any insurance policies. If, while any Obligations are outstanding, any return premiums, dividends, other amounts or proceeds are paid to Secured Party under such policies, Secured Party may at Secured Party's option take either or both of the following actions: (i) apply such return premiums, dividends, other amounts and proceeds in whole or in part to the payment of the unpaid installments of principal and interest on the Note in the inverse order of maturity or to the payment of satisfaction of any other obligations; or (ii) pay over such return premiums, dividends, other amounts and proceeds in whole or in part to Debtor for the purpose of repairing or replacing the Collateral destroyed or damaged, any return premiums, dividends, other amounts and proceeds so paid over by Secured Party to be secured by this Agreement.

10. *Fixtures.* It is the intention of Debtor and Secured Party that none of the Collateral shall become fixtures.

11. *Default.* If, while any Obligations are outstanding, any one or more of the following events of default shall occur:

(a) any representation made by Debtor is untrue or any warranty is not fulfilled;

(b) Debtor fails to pay any amounts due under any of the Obligations when due;

(c) Debtor fails to observe or perform any covenant, warranty or agreement to be performed by debtor under (i) this Agreement or (ii) under any other document executed by Debtor in connection with the Obligations;

(d) Debtor shall be in default under any obligation undertaken by Debtor which default has a material adverse effect on the financial condition of Debtor or on the value of the Collateral;

(e) Debtor or any guarantor of any of the Obligations is involved in any financial difficult as evidenced by:

(i) an assignment, composition or similar device for the benefit of creditors, or

(ii) inability to pay debts when due, or

(iii) an attachment or receivership of assets not dissolved within thirty (30) days, or

(iv) the filing by Debtor or any guarantor of a petition under any chapter of the Federal Bankruptcy Code or the institution of any other proceeding under any law relating to bankruptcy, bankruptcy reorganization, insolvency or relief of debtors, or

(v) the filing against Debtor or any guarantor of an involuntary petition under any chapter of the Federal Bankruptcy Code or the institution of any other proceeding under any law relating to bankruptcy, bankruptcy reorganization, insolvency or relief of debtors where such petition or proceeding is not dismissed within thirty (30) days from the date on which it is filed or instituted; then in each such event Secured Party may declare Debtor in default and exercise the Rights on Default as hereinafter defined.

12. *Rights on Default.* In the event of a default under this Agreement, Secured Party may:

(a) by written notice to Debtor declare the Obligations, or any of them, to be immediately due and payable without presentment, demand, protest or notice of any kind, all of which are hereby expressly waived;

(b) exercise the rights and remedies accorded a secured party by the Uniform Commercial Code or by any document securing the Obligations;

(c) perform any warranty, covenant or agreement which Debtor has failed to perform under this agreement;

(d) take any other action which Secured party deems necessary or desirable to protect the Collateral or the Security Interest.

No course of dealing or delay in accelerating the Obligations or in taking or failing to take any other action with respect to any event of default shall affect Secured Party's right to take such action at a later time. No waiver as to any one default shall affect Secured Party's rights upon any other default.

Secured Party may exercise any or all of its Rights on Default concurrently with or independently of and without regard to provisions of any other document which secures an Obligation.

After default, Debtor, upon demand by Secured Party, shall assemble the Collateral at Debtor's cost and make it available to Secured Party at a place to be designated by Secured Party.

The requirement of the Uniform Commercial Code that Secured Party give Debtor reasonable notice of any proposed sale of disposition of the Collateral shall be met if such notice is given to Debtor at least five (5) days before the time of such sale or disposition.

13. *Expenses.* Any payment made or expense incurred by Secured Party (including, without limitation, reasonable attorney's fees and disbursements) in connection with the preparation of this Agreement, any other document executed by Debtor in connection with the Obligations and any amendment thereto, or in connection with the exercise of any Right on Default shall be added to the indebtedness of Debtor to Secured Party, shall earn interest at the rate set forth in the Note, shall be payable upon demand and shall be secured by the Security Interest.

14. *Notices.* Any notice under this Agreement shall be in writing and shall be deemed delivered if mailed, postage prepaid, to a party at the principal place of business specified in this Agreement or such other address as may be specified by notice given after the date hereof.

15. *Successors and Assigns.* This Agreement shall inure to the benefit of and shall bind the heirs, executors, administrators, legal representatives, successors and assigns of the parties. The obligations of Debtor, if more than one, shall be joint and several.

16. *Interpretation.* Reference to the singular or the plural shall be deemed to include the other where the context requires. In particular, the use of the term "Debtor" in the singular shall include all debtors and the default of any debtor shall be deemed to be a default of all debtors.

17. *Governing Law.* This Agreement shall be governed by and construed under the laws of

      .

This Agreement shall have the effect of an instrument under seal.

BY: _____

BY: _____

State of   }
County of
On   before me,   ,
appeared
personally known to me (or proved to me on the basis of satisfactory evidence) to be the person(s) whose name(s) is/are subscribed to the within instrument and acknowledged to me that he/she/they executed the same in his/her/their authorized capacity(ies), and that by his/her/their signature(s) on the instrument the person(s), or the entity upon behalf of which the person(s) acted, executed the instrument.
WITNESS my hand and official seal.

_____
Signature of Notary   Affiant _____Known_____Produced ID
                                                        Type of ID _____
                                                                         (Seal)

PLEDGE AGREEMENT

KNOW ALL MEN BY THESE PRESENTS

I,   (Pledgor) of   ,
or valuable consideration paid, hereby DEPOSIT and PLEDGE with
s collateral security to secure the payment of a certain promissory note of even date in the original
rincipal amount of $ as issued to
y the undersigned, (hereinafter referred to as "DEBT"), and to secure the payment of any other direct
r indirect, primary or secondary liability, joint or several, or any renewals thereof, of the undersigned
o said Pledgee, due or to become due, or that may hereafter be contracted, and to secure any judgment
n any of the foregoing, the following described property:

             shares of the common stock of   represented by
Certificate No.   , and representing all the shares of said Corporation presently owned by the
undersigned.

Any addition to or substitutes for the foregoing security shall likewise be deemed pledged with
the Pledge hereof, as collateral security for said liabilities and included in the term security as used
herein.

The Pledge may assign or transfer said debt to any person, firm or corporation and deliver said
security, or any part thereof, to such assignee or transferee who shall thereupon become vested with
all rights and powers herein given to the Pledgee in respect thereof; and such assignor or transferor
shall thereafter be relieved and discharged from any responsibility or liability to the undersigned in
respect thereof.

Any deposits or other sums at any time credited by or due form the Pledgee to the undersigned
and any securities of other properties of the undersigned in the possession of the pledgee, whether in
safe keeping or otherwise, may at all times be held and treated as collateral security for the payment
of the said debt, an any other liabilities of the undersigned to the Pledgee hereof, and such deposits or
other sums may at any time be applied or set-off against the amount due or to become due on said
debt, or any other liability of the undersigned.

It is acknowledged that during the pendency of this pledge agreement, the Pledgor shall have all
rights to vote the stock, and shall be entitled to all dividends thereon.

The undersigned represent that they have a controlling interest in the corporation from which
said pledged stock is issued and they shall not vote for any further issue of stock of any class during
the pendency of this agreement, or if any further stock be issued, then it shall be delivered to the
Pledgee as additional collateral security hereunder.

Undersigned further warrants that during the pendency of this pledge agreement, that:

1. Undersigned as principal stockholder shall not issue any proxies on said pledged shares.

2. Undersigned shall not vote to:

    (a) Sell, transfer or convey assets of the Corporation out of the ordinary course of business

    (b) Remove or relocate the principal business location of the Corporation outside o

Upon nonpayment of said debt, or any liability above mentioned whenever due, or in any case the undersigned shall be adjudged a bankrupt or shall file a voluntary petition in bankruptcy or shall make a general assignment for the benefit of creditors or in case a petition be filed praying that the undersigned be adjudged a bankrupt, or a receiver of the undersigned's property shall be appointed by any court, the Pledgee may immediately sell the whole or any part of the security, with or without notice or advertisement, either at a public or private sale, at the option of the pledgee. The proceeds of the sale shall be applied (a) towards the payment of all expenses incurred by the Pledgee, including costs and expenses of collections, sale and deliver, and reasonable attorneys' fees, (b) towards payment of said debt, (c) towards the payment of any liabilities secured hereby, and (d) any balance then remaining to be paid to the undersigned. The Pledgee may bid and become purchaser at any such public sale, or at any private sale made through a stock exchange or Broker's Board, free from any right of redemption, which the undersigned hereby waives and releases and no other purchaser shall be responsible for the application of the purchase money. No delay of the Pledgee in exercising any right hereunder shall constitute waiver of such right. The Pledgee shall have the right to enforce any one or more of its remedies, whether or not herein specified, in whole or in part, successively or concurrently.

The Pledgee hereof may pay taxes, charges, assessments, liens or insurance premiums on the security or any part of it or otherwise protect the value thereof and the property represented thereby, and may charge against the security all expenditures so incurred, but the Pledgee hereof shall be under no duty or liability with respect to the collection of any security held hereunder or of any income thereon nor with respect the protection or preservation of any rights pertaining thereto beyond the safe custody of such security.

The Pledgee hereof may collect any part of said security by any lawful means. The term Pledgee shall mean and include any subsequent holder or transferee.

IN WITNESS WHEREOF,

I hereunder set my hand and seal this   day of   ,   (year).

_____   _____
Pledgor   Witness

COLLATERAL ASSIGNMENT OF LEASE

Assignment Agreement made this   day of   ,   (year) by and
etween   , a   corporation with a usual place
f business at   ,   ,   ,
ereinafter referred to as Assignor) and   , a
orporation with a usual place of business at   ,   ,
                        (herein referred to as Assignee).

WITNESSETH:

1. For value received, Assignor hereby grants, transfers and assigns to Assignee
the right title and interest of the Assignor in and to (and all Assignor's rights under and in) that
certain lease dated   ,   (year) between ASSIGNOR as original
tenant and   , as Landlord, for the premises known
and numbered   ,   ,   ,
which Lease, Assignor presently holds and a copy of which is annexed hereto as Exhibit "A."

2. Assignor further grants, transfers and assigns to Assignee its full right of occupancy of the premises for the term of years set forth in said lease, and for any extension thereafter so long as the debt described below shall remain unpaid and shall be due and owing.

3. This assignment is made to secure the following:

a. Payment of the principal sum and interest evidenced by a Promissory Note, and any amendments, extensions or renewals thereof in the original sum of
                ($) Dollars made by Assignor in favor of Assignee, and
dated   herein referred to as the Note and secured by a chattel mortgage in the restaurant equipment and fixtures located at the above described premises.

b. Payment of all other sums, with interest, which may become due and payable to Assignee under this Agreement or under the Note and Security Agreement.

c. Assignee's performance and discharge of every obligation and agreement of Assignee under this Assignment or under the Note and Security Agreement.

4. Assignor agrees:

a. To observe and perform all obligations imposed on Lessee under the Lease hereby assigned and to indemnify Assignee from the consequences of any failure to do so.

b. To pay all rent and any other charges accruing under the Lease in a timely fashion.

c. To preserve the subject property free and clear of all liens and encumbrances, except as otherwise agreed by parties hereto.

d. Not to execute any other assignment of Lessee's interest in the Lease.

e. Not to alter, terminate or modify the terms of the lease or waive any renewal or option permitted by the terms of the lease without the prior written consent of Assignee.

f. Not to terminate, cancel or surrender the Lease, so as to cause a termination or changing of the obligations of Lessee.

5. Assignee shall not be liable for any loss sustained by Assignor resulting from Assignee's failure to let the premises or from any other act or omission of Assignee in managing the premises, unless such loss is caused by the willful conduct or bad faith of Assignee. Assignee shall fur-

ther not be obligated to perform or discharge any obligation or duty under the lease, or under this assignment. Assignor agrees to indemnify Assignee for any liability, loss or damage which may be incurred under the lease or by reason of this assignment. In the event Assignee incur any such liability above referred to or, in defense of any such claims or demand, the amount thereof, including costs and reasonable attorneys' fees shall be secured by this assignment, and Assignor shall reimburse Assignee immediately therefor upon the demand of Assignee. Further this assignment shall not make Assignee responsible for any waste committed on the property by other parties, or for any dangerous or defective condition of the premises, or for any negli gence in the management, repair or control of the premises.

6. Nothing contained in the assignment, nor any act done or omitted by Assignee pursuant to the terms of this assignment shall be deemed a waiver by Assignee of any of the rights or remedies under the Note and Security Agreement, and this assignment is executed without prejudice to any rights or remedies possessed by Assignee under the terms of any other instruments referred to herein. The right of Assignee to collect the secured principal, interest and other indebtedness and to enforce any other security may be exercised by Assignee prior or subsequent to any action taken under this Assignment.

7. Until the indebtedness secured hereby shall have been paid in full, Assignors covenant and agree to keep and perform all their obligations under the Lease.

8. Upon the payment in full of all indebtedness secured hereby, this Assignment shall become and be void and of no effect, but the affidavit of any officer of the Assignor showing any part of said indebtedness to remain unpaid shall be and constitute exclusive evidence of the validity, effectiveness and continuing force of this Assignment, and any person may and is hereby authorized to rely thereon.

9. This assignment applies to, inures to the benefit of, and binds the parties hereto, their successors and assigns.

10. The term "Lease" as used herein means the Lease hereby assigned or any extension or renewal thereof or any Lease subsequently executed by Assignors covering the Premises or any part thereof.

IN WITNESS WHEREOF, Assignors and Assignee have executed this Collateral Assignment of lease as of the day and year first above written.

By: _____

By: _____

Assented to:

Lessor:

By: _____

LETTER OF INTENT

Attention:

Dear

Please be advised that we represent   relative to his/her interest in acquiring the business known as   ("   "). We understand that   has been introduced to this business through your office.

My client is interested in acquiring the business on the following terms:

1. The transfer shall be through a sale of assets (not shares in the seller corporation). The assets would consist of all inventory, fixtures, furniture, equipment and the name and goodwill of the business.

2. The seller would retain all cash on hand, accounts and notes receivable, prepaid expenses, motor vehicles, tax rebates and any pending claims owed by the corporation.

3. The offered purchase price for the business is $ based on an inventory level of $ wholesale cost at the time of transfer. In the event the inventory is less or more than $, the difference shall be added or subtracted from the purchase price.

4. We would expect the final documents to reflect that the purchase price shall for tax purposes be allocated:

$ Inventory (or as adjusted)

$ Fixtures and equipment

$ Goodwill

$ Total purchase price

5. The proposed purchase price would be paid in the following manner:

$ Cash down payment (tendered as a deposit).

$ Deposit upon signing the formal agreement.

$ By the assumption of the seller's existing liabilities at the time of closing.

$ to be financed by seller, payable over five years with 12 percent interest. The note would be guaranteed by
and secured by a first mortgage on assets, and an assignment of lease, assented to by the landlord

6. Any adjustment based on any increase or decrease in either inventory or liabilities shall be added or subtracted from the note balance, and not the down payment.

7. Except for the liabilities expressly to be assumed, the assets shall be sold free and clear of all claims, debts, liens or other liabilities with   receiving good and marketable title.

8. We shall expect the seller,   , to agree to a non-compete agreement preventing them from engaging in the retail shoe business for   years within   miles of the present business address.

9. This offer is expressly conditional upon:

(a) The buyer obtaining a lease on the premises on such terms, rents and conditions as he deems acceptable.

(b) The buyer's accountant verifying further additional information and his satisfaction of same.

(c) Our entering into an agreement on terms, satisfactory to us within 10 days of acceptance of this offer.

In the event these conditions are not fully satisfied, this offer, or any subsequent formal agreement, may be terminated by the buyer and all deposits shall be promptly refunded.

10. We enclose the buyer's certified check for $ to be held in escrow by your firm pending the closing and transfer.

If this offer is acceptable to the seller, please have him signify by signing where indicated and return a signed copy to our office within 10 days of above date. You should consider the offer withdrawn if we do not hear from you within this time. Upon acceptance, we propose to immediately enter into a formal purchase and sales agreement on these terms.

We understand that all brokerage fees shall be paid by the seller and that an acceptable date of closing would be on or about   ,   (year).

I appreciate your cooperation in bringing this offer to the attention of the seller

Very truly yours,

_____

The foregoing offer is accepted on its terms:

By:

_____

_____

CONFIDENTIALITY AGREEMENT

AGREEMENT and acknowledgement between   (Company)
nd   (undersigned).

WHEREAS, the Company agrees to furnish the undersigned certain confidential information
elating to the affairs of the Company for purposes of evaluating the business of the Company for
urposes of prospective purchase and acquisition by the undersigned, and

WHEREAS, the undersigned agrees to review, examine, inspect or obtain such information only
or the purposes described above, and to otherwise hold such information confidential pursuant to the
erms of this agreement,

BE IT KNOWN, that the company has or shall furnish to the undersigned certain confidential
nformation, as set forth on attached list, and may further allow the undersigned the right to inspect
he business of the Company and/or interview employees or representatives of the Company, all on
he following conditions:

1. The undersigned agrees to hold all confidential or proprietary information or trade secrets
"information") in trust and confidence and agrees that it shall be used only for the contemplated
urpose, shall not be used for any other purpose or disclosed to any third party.

2. No copies will be made or retained of any written information supplied.

3. At the conclusion of our discussions, or upon demand by the Company, all information,
ncluding written notes, photographs, memoranda, or notes taken by you shall be returned to us.

4. This information shall not be disclosed to any employee or consultant unless they agree to
execute and be bound by the terms of this agreement.

5. It is understood that the undersigned shall have no obligation with respect to any information
known by the undersigned or generally known within the industry prior to date of this agreement, or
becomes common knowledge within the industry thereafter.

Dated:

By: _____
    Authorized Officer

    _____

INDEMNITY AGREEMENT ON NON-ASSUMED OBLIGATIONS

TO WHOM IT MAY CONCERN:

As an inducement for your entering into an agreement to acquire assets of

, , ,

(hereinafter "Corporation"), and in further consideration of your waiver of compliance with The Bulk Sales Act, I the undersigned as the principal of the Corporation, do hereby agree:

1. That I shall cause all known and liquidated debts of the Corporation to be paid from the proceeds of sale by making full payment to all creditors holding non-disputed claims within twenty (20) days of closing date. In accordance therewith I hereby agree that all proceeds of sale shall be deposited in escrow with your attorney , who shall have full authority to issue checks as we may direct.

2. I further acknowledge our agreement to defend against and otherwise fully indemnify and save you harmless from any actual or alleged liability or claim arising from the corporation. In accordance thereto, in the event any such claim is made, then you shall provide us reasonably timely notice of same. I shall thereafter defend against said claim at our own expense. In the event I shall fail to so defend, or you shall otherwise incur any loss, including but not limited to attachment, or other sequestration on any asset sold, then you may upon prior notice to us pay, settle or otherwise discharge said asserted claim. I shall thereinafter within thirty (30) days fully reimburse you for all sums expended in discharging said claim together with reasonable attorneys' fees required in your defending against said claim.

3. In the further event I shall be in breach of this agreement, I agree to pay all reasonable costs and attorneys' fees necessary for the enforcement hereunder.

4. This indemnity agreement shall not extend to certain obligations expressly to be assumed by you pursuant to Article of a certain purchase and sale agreement between us, and shall not apply to asserted claims for which adequate insurance coverage is available. This agreement, however, shall otherwise be unlimited as to amount and duration.

5. This agreement shall be binding upon, and inure to the benefit of the parties, their successors, assigns and personal representatives.

Signed under seal this day of , (year).

_____

F10

COVENANT NOT TO COMPETE

For   and other good consideration, I,
undersigned"), do hereby agree that I shall not directly or indirectly compete with the business of
with an address at   .

The term "not compete" as herein used shall mean that the undersigned shall not, in any
capacity, directly or indirectly engage in the business of a   ,
whether as an owner, partner, officer, director, employee, agent, consultant, investor, lender or
stockholder (except as a minority stockholder of a public corporation).

This covenant shall remain in full force and effect for   (   )
years from date hereof, and extend only to a radius of   (   )
miles from   .

In the event of any alleged breach, the undersigned shall be provided written notice of same
and be allowed   (   ) days to cure. Thereafter, and unless fully cured,
or its lawful successors and assigns shall have full legal and equitable
relief, without requirement for posting bond as a condition for injunctive relief; the remedies herein
being cumulative and not necessarily successive. The breach by one of the undersigned shall equally
constitute a breach by the other and their liability shall be joint and several.

Signed under seal this   day of   ,   (year).

_____

BILL OF SALE

FOR VALUE RECEIVED, and pursuant to a certain agreement between the parties, BE I KNOWN, that   , an   corporatic with a usual place of business at   ,
(hereinafter "Seller"), does hereby sell, transfer, convey and assign forev unto   . another   corporation, and i successors and assigns (hereinafter "Buyer"), each and all of the following assets and propertie located on, or used in connection with the Seller's business, being more particularly described as:

(a)   All merchandise, inventory, goods for resale and supplies.

(b)   All furniture, fixtures, equipment, leasehold improvements and appurtenances an accessories thereto as more particularly set forth in Exhibit C, to said purchase and sal agreement, and as otherwise contained.

(c)   All goodwill, rights to the name "   ," customer list trade secrets and transfer of telephone numbers.

The aforesaid assets are sold subject to such terms, conditions, warranties and disclaimers as se forth within the agreement between the parties which provisions are herein incorporated by referenc and intended to survive acceptance of this bill of sale.

Provided, nevertheless, that Seller hereby warrants that it has good and sufficient title to sai assets, that said assets are being sold free and clear of all liens, encumbrances, liabilities or advers claims thereto, and that Seller warrants to Buyer good and marketable title to each and all of sai assets and shall defend against and fully indemnify and save harmless Buyer from any claims advers thereto.

Signed under seal this   day of   ,   (year).

_____

BY: _____
            Authorized Officer

BULK SALES AFFIDAVIT

I, _____ , the undersigned, being President of

_____ , (Seller), and being of lawful age, being first duly sworn, on oath state:

1. That the undersigned executes this affidavit on behalf of the Seller under a certain contract
for the sale of assets from Seller to _____ (Buyer), on this date
_____ , _____ (year).

2. That this affidavit is furnished pursuant to Article 6 of the Uniform Commercial Code, and is
provided to the above named Buyer in connection with the sale described under said contract.

3. That the following is a true, complete and accurate list of all the creditors of Seller, and to the
knowledge of the undersigned, assert or claim to assert one or more claims against the Seller, together
with the correct business address of each such creditor or claimant and the amounts due and owing or
otherwise claimed. (Attach list naming creditors, their address and claimed amount due.)

Signed under seal this _____ day of _____ , _____ (year).

BY: _____

State of _____ }
County of _____
On _____ before me, _____ ,
appeared _____
personally known to me (or proved to me on the basis of satisfactory evidence) to be the person(s) whose name(s)
is/are subscribed to the within instrument and acknowledged to me that he/she/they executed the same in his/her/their
authorized capacity(ies), and that by his/her/their signature(s) on the instrument the person(s), or the entity upon
behalf of which the person(s) acted, executed the instrument.
WITNESS my hand and official seal.

_____
Signature of Notary

Affiant _____ Known _____ Produced ID
Type of ID _____
(Seal)

BALANCE SHEET

Company_____

Year Ending _____, _____

Assets

Liabilities

Current Assets
____ Cash
____ Accounts receivable _____
      less allowance
      doubtful accounts _____
      Net realizable value
____ Inventory
____ Temporary investment
____ Prepaid expenses

____ **Total Current Assets**
____ **Long term investments**

Fixed Assets
____ Land

____ Buildings _____ at
      cost, less accumulated
      depreciation of_____
____ Net book value

____ Equipment _____ at
      cost, less accumulated
      depreciation of_____
      Net book value
____ Furniture/Fixtures _____ at
      cost, less accumulated
      depreciation of_____
      Net book value

____ **Total Net Fixed Assets**
____ Other assets
____ **TOTAL ASSETS**

Current Liabilities
____ Accounts payable
____ Short-term notes
      Current portion
____ of long-term notes
____ Interest payable
____ Taxes payable
____ Accrued payroll
____ **Total Current Liabilities**

____ **Equity**
____ Total Owner's equity
      (proprietorship)

            or
____ (Name's) equity
____ (Name's) equity
      (partnership)
____ Total partner's equity
      Shareholder's equity
      (corporation)
____ Capital stock
____ Capital paid-in in excess of par
____ Retained earnings
____ Total shareholder's equity
____ **TOTAL LIABILITIES AND EQUITY**

BUSINESS ANALYSIS CHART

Company Strengths and Weaknesses

Functions	Strong +	Average 0	Weak –	Major Strengths and/or Weaknesses
General administration				
Marketing				
Finance				
Human resources				
Engineering				
Operations				
Production				
Purchasing				
Distribution				
Research				
Other				
Other				

BUSINESS SCREENING ANALYSIS

	YES	NO	UNCERTAIN
1. I have the background and experience necessary to own and operate this type of business.	____	____	____
2. The business meets my investment requirements. I have enough money to do it right.	____	____	____
3. This business meets my income requirements. I can make enough money and also pay any debt service.	____	____	____
4. I feel comfortable with this type of business. The chemistry is right.	____	____	____
5. The business matches my "people orientation."	____	____	____
6. There is good growth in this industry.	____	____	____
7. The risk factor is acceptable.	____	____	____
8. My family and spouse agree that this is the type of business to enter.	____	____	____
9. This business provides the status that I need.	____	____	____
10. This business fits in with my lifestyle requirements.	____	____	____
11. I have investigated a sufficient number of businesses of this type.	____	____	____
12. My professional advisors agree this is a good acquisition.	____	____	____

F1

BUSINESS VALUATION WORKSHEET

Business Name _____   Year End _____

1.   CAPITALIZATION VALUE
Company profits before taxes _____ |_____|_____|
Depreciation _____ |
Interest expense_____ |
Owners' wage _____ |
Reconstructed expenses _____   Reason for expense change _____
    1. excess T/E _____   _____
    2. excess payroll_____   _____
    3. expenses that should be cap'd ___   _____
    4. non-bus. ventures _____   _____
    5. one time charge-offs _____   _____
    6. owner's personal items _____   _____
        a. _____   _____
        b. _____   _____
        c. _____   _____
    7. other _____   _____
        a. _____   _____
        b. _____   _____
Total available income _____
Less: Owner's fair wage _____
Reconstructed cash flow
25% capitalization value (multiply RCF by 4)
20% capitalization value (multiply RCF by 5)
Ending inventory level

2.   FAIR MARKET VALUE OF THE ASSETS
Cash (if applicable) _____
Accounts receivable (if applicable)____
Inventory _____
Furniture and fixtures _____
Equipment _____
Franchise or license_____
Other
    Total fair market value of assets
If asset sale: add total FMV assets
to reconstruct cash flow for business selling price

3.   CAPITAL STOCK VALUE
Accounts payable _____
Notes payable _____
Notes payable–owner _____
Accrued expenses _____
Withheld items & income taxes ____
Other liabilities _____
    Total liabilities
Subtract total liabilities from
asset sale price for capital stock value

BUYER'S LETTER TO PROSPECTIVE SELLERS

Date:

Dear

We want to acquire a   firm within the
area, with sales between   and   .
We prefer one that specializes in   , however, we will consider
comparable opportunities.

We are principals and not business brokers. We have capital and financing and can close immediately on the right situation.

If you are interested in selling, please call us at your earliest convenience. You have our assurance that all matters shall be held in strict confidence. Our business card is enclosed for future reference if you have no present interest in selling. Of course, we would greatly appreciate your directing this letter to any of your colleagues whose business matching our needs may be on the market.

Very truly yours,

BUYER PROFILE

Name _____

Address _____

_____

Telephone _____ Fax _____

Hours to call _____ E-mail _____

Type business desired

_____

_____

Approximate sales

_____

_____

Geographic area

_____

_____

Price range

_____

_____

Other business requirements

_____

_____

Other business types acceptable

_____

_____

Cash available

_____

_____

Financing available

_____

Other

_____

_____

BUYER'S PROFITABILITY ANALYSIS

NET PROFIT $ _____

ADD BACK
   Depreciation $ _____
   Amortization $ _____
   Debt Service (loan interest) $ _____
   Income tax $ _____
   Owner's salary $ _____
   Manager's salary $ _____
   Personal expenses $ _____
    Promotion $ _____
    Insurance $ _____
    Travel and entertainment $ _____
    Auto $ _____
    Other (specify) $ _____

EXPENSES BUYERS MAY ELIMINATE
   Equipment rental $ _____
   Discounts and refunds $ _____
   Bad debt $ _____
   Donations $ _____
   Extra employees $ _____
   Other (specify) $ _____

ADD: TOTAL ADJUSTMENTS
TOTAL ANNUAL "TRUE NET PROFIT"
LESS BUYER'S DEBTS:
   Debt service payments $ _____
   Equipment rental payments $ _____
   New loan payment $ _____
   Other (specify) $ _____

LESS TOTAL ADJUSTMENTS $ _____

"NET CASH" AVAILABLE TO BUYERS $ _____

CAPITAL REQUIREMENTS ANALYSIS

Down payment $ _____

Additional inventory $ _____

Renovation expense $ _____

New fixtures and equipment $ _____

Utility deposits $ _____

Licenses, permits and fees $ _____

Legal and accounting fees $ _____

Adjustments due at closing $ _____

Advertising launch $ _____

Working capital requirements $ _____

Other

_____ $ _____

_____ $ _____

_____ $ _____

TOTAL CAPITAL REQUIREMENTS $_____

CASH FLOW/DEBT SERVICE ANALYSIS

(Year)   _____ _____ _____ _____

Total Income   _____ _____ _____ _____

Disbursements

  Cost of sales   _____ _____ _____ _____

  Total expense   _____ _____ _____ _____
  (minus depreciation and interest on loans)

  Capital expenditures   _____ _____ _____ _____

  Other   _____ _____ _____ _____

Total disbursements   _____ _____ _____ _____

Total cash flow before debt service   _____ _____ _____ _____

Annual payments on debt service   _____ _____ _____ _____

Net cash flow after debt service   _____ _____ _____ _____

CASH FLOW STATEMENT

(Four year projections)

Item				
RECEIPTS				
Cash sales				
Loans				
Other				
TOTAL RECEIPTS				
DISBURSEMENTS				
Direct materials or purchases				
Labor				
Equipment				
Salaries				
Rent				
Insurance				
Advertising				
Taxes				
Loan payments				
Other				
TOTAL DISBURSEMENTS				
NET CASH FLOW				
BEGINNING BALANCE				
ENDING BALANCE				

CHART OF MONTHLY SALES

_____ to _____

1st	2nd	3rd	4th	5th	6th	7th	8th	9th	10th	11th	12th

Month by month, _____

COLLATERAL VALUES
FOR BUSINESS FINANCING

Business assets pledged (net of prior encumbrances)	Fair market value	Auction or liquidation value
Accounts receivable	$	$
Inventory	$	$
Fixtures and equipment	$	$
Motor vehicles	$	$
Real estate	$	$
Other	$	$
SUBTOTALS:	$ _____	$ _____
Real estate (less prior mortgages)		
Securities and stocks		
Others:		
	$ _____	$ _____
SUBTOTALS:	$ _____	$ _____
TOTALS:	$ _____	$ _____

COMPETITOR ANALYSIS

Major Competitors	Sales Volume ($000)	Growth Rate	Competitive Areas	Strengths	Weaknesses

FACILITY & EQUIPMENT ANALYSIS

Location	Use	Size (sq. ft.)	Capacity	Utilization (%)	Equipment	Capacity/ Age	Utilization (%)

FINANCIAL PERFORMANCE ANALYSIS

KEY INDICATORS				
Income data				
Net sales				
Cost of goods sold				
Gross profit				
Net profit before taxes				
Net profit after taxes				
Asset/liability data				
Accounts receivable				
Inventory				
Total assets				
Accounts payable				
Short-term debt				
Long-term debt				
Total liabilities				
Net worth				
Ratios				
Current				
Total debt to total assets				
Collection period				
Net sales to inventory				
Net profit margin after taxes				
Return on net worth				

FINANCIAL COMPARISON ANALYSIS

	INDUSTRY			COMPANY		
Assets						
Accts & notes receivable						
Inventory						
Total current						
Fixed assets (net)						
TOTAL ASSETS						
Liabilities						
Accts & notes payable						
Total current						
Long-term debt						
Net worth						
TOTAL LIABILITIES						
& NET WORTH						
Income data						
Net sales						
Cost of goods sold						
Gross profit						
Operating expenses						
Operating profit						
All other expenses (net)						
PROFIT BEFORE TAXES						
Ratios						
Current						
Total debt/total assets						
Total debt/tangible net worth						
Collection period days						
Net sales/inventory						
Total assets turnover						
Gross profit margin						
Operating profit margin						
Return on net worth						

FOUR YEAR BALANCE SHEET

ITEM				
Current assets				
Cash				
Accounts receivable less allowance for doubtful accounts				
Net accounts receivable				
Notes receivable				
Inventory				
Prepaid expenses				
Other				
TOTAL CURRENT ASSETS				
Fixed assets				
Land				
Buildings				
Equipment				
TOTAL NET FIXED ASSETS				
Other assets:				
TOTAL ASSETS				
Current liabilities				
Accounts payable				
Notes payable				
Accrued payroll				
Taxes payable				
Other				
TOTAL CURRENT LIABILITIES				
Long-term liabilities				
Equity				
Withdrawals				
Net equity				
TOTAL LIABILITY & EQUITY				

FOUR YEAR INCOME STATEMENTS

ITEM				
Revenues				
Sales allowances				
Net Revenues				
Cost of goods sold				
Gross margin				
Expenses				
Selling				
Salaries				
Advertising				
Other				
General/Administrative				
Salaries				
Employee benefits				
Professional services				
Rent				
Insurance				
Depreciation				
Amortization				
Office supplies				
Interest				
Utilities				
Bad debt/doubtful accounts				
Other				
TOTAL EXPENSES				
Net income before taxes				
Provision for taxes				
Net income after taxes				
Prior period adjustments				
Net increase/(decrease) to retained earnings				

INCOME STATEMENT

Company_____

For_____(month) and year to date ended _____, _____

(\$000)

	Current Month		Year to Date	
	Amount	% of Sales	Amount	% of Sales
REVENUE				
Gross sales	_____	_____	_____	_____
Less sales returns and allowances	_____	_____	_____	_____
Net sales	_____	_____	_____	_____
Cost of sales	_____	_____	_____	_____
Beginning inventory	_____	_____	_____	_____
Plus purchases (retailer) or	_____	_____	_____	_____
Plus cost of goods	_____	_____	_____	_____
manufactured (manufacturer)	_____	_____	_____	_____
Total goods available	_____	_____	_____	_____
Less ending inventory	_____	_____	_____	_____
Total cost of goods sold	_____	_____	_____	_____
Gross profit (gross margin)	_____	_____	_____	_____
OPERATING EXPENSES				
Selling				
Salaries and wages	_____	_____	_____	_____
Commissions	_____	_____	_____	_____
Advertising	_____	_____	_____	_____
Depreciation (e.g., on delivery vans)	_____	_____	_____	_____
Others (detail)	_____	_____	_____	_____
Total selling expenses	_____	_____	_____	_____
General/Administrative	_____	_____	_____	_____
Salaries and wages	_____	_____	_____	_____
Employee benefits	_____	_____	_____	_____
Insurance	_____	_____	_____	_____
Depreciation (e.g. on equipment)	_____	_____	_____	_____
Total general/administrative expenses	_____	_____	_____	_____
Total operating expenses	_____	_____	_____	_____
Operating income	_____	_____	_____	_____
Other revenue and expenses	_____	_____	_____	_____
Net income before taxes	_____	_____	_____	_____
Taxes on income	_____	_____	_____	_____
Net income after taxes	_____	_____	_____	_____
Extraordinary gain or loss	_____	_____	_____	_____
Income tax on extraordinary gain	_____	_____	_____	_____
NET INCOME (NET PROFIT)	_____	_____	_____	_____

OFFERING CIRCULAR

Description: _____
_____
_____
_____

Location: _____
_____
_____
_____

Sales: _____
_____
_____

Profits: _____
_____
_____

Asking price: _____
_____

Financing: _____
_____
_____

Management: _____
_____
_____

Contact: _____
_____
_____
_____

PERFORMANCE TRENDS

(Five year analysis)

Sales ($000)					
Net income after taxes ($000)					
Return on sales (%)					
Return on net assets (%)					
Return on equity (%)					
Current ratio					
Debt to equity ratio					

PERSONAL BALANCE SHEET

Assets   ## Liabilities

____ Cash   _____ Loans to banks
____ Stocks or other   _____ Loans to others
____negotiable securities   _____ Real estate loans
____ (market value)   _____ Other debts
____ Notes receivable   _____
____ Value of real estate   _____
____ (market value)   _____ Credit cards and retail stores
____   Home
____   Other   _____ **Total Liabilities**
____ Automobiles
____ Cash value of life insurance _____ **Total Net Worth**
____ Personal assets   _____ **Total Liabilities Plus Net Worth**
____ Personal

____ **Total Assets**

Capital Available
for Business Investment

Sources of cash   Amount
(e.g., savings, stocks, friends, relatives, equity in property, etc.)

_____   _____
_____   _____
_____   _____
_____   _____
_____   _____
_____   _____
_____   _____
_____   _____
_____   _____

                    TOTAL   _____

PROJECTED QUARTERLY CASH FLOW

Year:				
ITEM	1st Qtr.	2nd Qtr.	3rd Qtr.	4th Qtr.
Income				
Cash sales				
Loans				
Other				
TOTAL INCOME				
Disbursements				
Materials				
Direct labor				
Equipment				
Salaries				
Rent				
Insurance				
Advertising				
Taxes				
Loan payments				
Other				
TOTAL DISBURSEMENTS				
Net cash flow				
Beginning cash balance				
Ending cash balance				

PROJECTED INCOME STATEMENT

ITEM	Seller's Actual		Buyer's Projected	
	$000	%	$000	%
Revenues				
Sales Allowances				
Net revenues				
Cost of goods sold				
Gross margin				
Expenses				
Selling				
Salaries				
Advertising				
Other				
General/administrative				
Salaries				
Employee benefits				
Professional services				
Rent				
Insurance				
Depreciation				
Amortization				
Office supplies				
Interest				
Utilities				
Bad debt/doubtful accounts				
Other				
TOTAL EXPENSES				
Net Income before taxes				
Provisions for taxes				
Net income after taxes				
Prior period adjustments				
Net increase/ (decrease) to retained earnings				

Glossary of useful terms

Ac-As

Actuarial Method

The method of determining loan-repayment amounts based on the principles of compound interest; used by financial institutions.

Allocation

The process of distributing an expense to a number of items of areas.

Amortization

A reduction in a debt or fund by periodic payments covering interest and part of the principal.

Annuity

A series of equal payments over a period of time.

Assessed Valuation

The taxable value of a property.

Asset, Current

An asset that is either currently in the form of cash or is expected to be converted into cash within a short period, usually one year.

Asset, Fixed

Tangible property of relatively long life that generally is used in the production of goods and services.

Asset, Fixed, Gain (Or Loss) On The Disposition Of

Difference between net book value and amount actually realized from sale.

As-B

Asset, Net Book Value of

Cost less accumulated depreciation.

Assets

Everything a company owns or is. due to it; current assets, such as cash, investments, money due, materials and inventories; fixed assets, such as buildings and machinery and intangible assets, such as patents and goodwill. Property or property right owned by the business which is valuable either because it will be converted into cash or because it is expected to benefit future operations and was acquired at a measurable cost.

Authorized Stock

The maximum number of shares allowed by a corporation's charter.

Balance Sheet

A statement showing the nature and amount of a company's assets, liabilities and capital on a given date. In dollar amounts, the balance sheet shows what the company owned, what it owed and the ownership interest in the company of its stockholders. A consolidated balance sheet is one showing the financial condition of a corporation and its subsidiaries.

Base Year

A year chosen for comparison of prices as the 100 percent or normal year from which index numbers are computed.

Bond

A written promise to pay the holder a sum of money at a certain time (more than one year after issue) at a stated rate 0 interest. Generally issued in multiples of $1,000. A debt due in less than one year from date of issue is usually called a note.

Book Value

Book value of a stock is determined from a company's records by adding all assets (generally excluding such intangibles as goodwill), then deducting all debts and other liabilities, plus the liquidation price of any preferred issue. The sum arrived at is divided by the number of common shares outstanding and the result is book value per common share. Book value of the assets of a company or a security may have little or no significant relationship to market value.

Ca-Co

Capital

The amount that an individual partner, or stockholder has invested in his business; net worth of a business; the owner's (owners) claim to his (their) assets.

Capital Stock

All shares representing ownership of a business, including preferred and common.

Capitalization

Total amount of the various securities issued by a corporation. Capitalization may include bond, debentures and preferred and common stock. Bonds are usually carried on the books of the issuing company in terms of their par or face value. Preferred and common shares may be carried in terms of par or stated value. Stated value may be an arbitrary figure decided upon by the directors or may represent the amount received by the company from the sale of the securities at the time of issuance.

Cash Discount

A reduction of 1 - 3 percent in the amount due the seller on a purchase, granted for early payment.

Cash Flow

Reported net income of a corporation plus amounts charged off, such as depreciation and charges to reserves (which are bookkeeping deductions and not paid out in actual dollars), plus the decrease in accounts receivable or less the increase in accounts receivable for the period.

Charter

A formal document, issued by the state, permitting the establishment of a corporation.

Collateral

Securities or other property pledged by a borrower to secure repayment of a loan.

Co-Cu

Common Stock

Securities that represent an ownership interest in a corporation. If the company also has issued preferred stock, both common and preferred have ownership rights. However, the preferred normal has prior claim on dividends and in the event of liquidation, on assets as well. Claims of both common and preferred stockholders are junior to claims of bondholders or other creditors of the company. Common stockholders assume the greater risk, but generally exercise the greater control and may gain the greater regard in the form of dividends and capital appreciation.

Convertible

A bond, debenture or preferred share that may be exchanged by the owners for common stock or another security, usually of the same company, in accordance with the terms of the issue.

Corporation

Entity or organization created by operation of law with rights of doing business essentially the same as those of an individual. The entity has continuous existence regardless of that of its owners, and limits liability of owners to the amount invested in the organization. The entity ceases to exist only is dissolved according to proper legal process.

Cost of Goods Sold

The price paid for the merchandise that has been sold by a trading business; Example: Beginning inventory minus net purchases minus ending inventory equals cost of goods sold.

Credit Entry

An entry on the right-hand side of an account; the record of a decrease in any asset account; the record of an increase in an equity account.

Current Assets

Those assets of a company that are reasonably expected to be realized in cash, or sold, or consumed during the normal operating cycle of the business. These include: Cash, U.S. government bonds, receivables, inventories, and money due usually within one year.

Current Liabilities

Money owed and payable by a company, usually within one year.

Cu-E

Current Ratio

The comparison of current assets to current liabilities; standard is 2: 1; total current assets divided by total current liabilities.

Depreciation

Charges against earnings to write off the cost, less salvage value, of an asset over its estimated useful life. It is a bookkeeping entry and does not represent any cash outlay or any funds earmarked for the purpose.

Dividend

The payment designated by the board of directors to be distributed pro-rata among the shares outstanding. On preferred shares, it is generally a fixed amount. On common shares, the dividend varies with the fortunes of the company and the amount of cash on hand, and may be omitted at the discretion of the directors if business is poor or if they determine to withhold earnings to invest in plant and equipment, research and development and so on. Sometimes a company will pay a dividend out of past earnings even if it is not currently operating at a profit.

Earnings Per Share

Net earnings divided by the number of shares outstanding.

Earnings, Retained

A cumulative increase in the stockholder's equity as a result of company operations.

Equity

The ownership interest of common and preferable stockholders in a company.

Expense

A decrease in owners' equity resulting from the operation of the business.

Expense, Accrued

A liability account arising from expenses that are incurred prior to the related expenditure. Example: Accrued wages.

E-J

Expense, Non-operating

Expense not related to company's business operations.

Expense, Prepaid

An expense recognized after a relevant expenditure; an expense for future benefits.

FICA (Federal Insurance Contributions Act) Tax

A required payroll deduction, the amount of which must be matched by the employer, that provides for old-age pensions, survivors' benefits, disability payments and Medicare.

Fifo

The first-in, first-out method of inventory valuation, which assumes that the goods that enter inventory first are the first to be sold.

Financial Statement

A formal document stating the results of business activity.

Fixed Asset

An asset whose life will extend beyond the next business activity.

Fixed Charges

A company's expenses, such as bond interest, that it has agreed to pay, whether or not earned.

Invested Fund, Return On

Net income divided by either (1) funds invested by a stockholder or (2) funds invested by stockholders and long-term creditors.

Issued Stock

Stock that has been sold by the corporation for whom the stock was authorized.

Journal

Preliminary records of transaction, kept in chronological order.

L-M

Liabilities

All the claims against a corporation. Liabilities include accounts and wages and salaries payable, dividends declared payable, accrued taxes payable, and fixed or long-term liabilities, such as mortgage bonds, debentures and bank loans.

Liability, Current

Obligation that becomes due within a short time, usually one year.

Lifo

The last-in-first-out method of inventory valuation which assumes that the goods that enter inventory last are the first to be sold.

Liquid Assets

Those assets easily convertible into cash; Example: Marketable securities, receivables and cash itself.

Liquidity

A measure of the quality and adequacy of current assets to meet current obligations as they come due.

Long-Term Liability

A liability due at a time after the next business year.

Loss, Net

Excess of total expenses over total revenues in a given period.

Maker

The person signing a promissory note; the giver of the note.

Market Value of Stock

The price at which stock is sold by a stockholder to a third party.

Markup

The amount added to cost to arrive at the original retail price expenses minus desired profit.

N-O

Net Asset Value

The worth of a share of stock, determined by dividing the net worth of the corporation by the number of outstanding shares.

Net Profit (Loss)

Profit remaining after deducting all operating expenses, gross profit minus operating expenses.

Net Worth

Total assets less amounts due creditors; it includes both capital stock and surplus.

Note

A written promise to repay a loan.

Note Receivable

A debt that is evidenced by a note or other written acknowledgement.

Obsolescence

Loss of value of a fixed asset arising because improved assets become available.

Outstanding Stock

Stock in the hands of stockholders: Stock that is issued but not re-acquired by the issuing corporation.

Overhead Rate

Method of allocating overhead to the various products manufactured.

Owners, Majority

Owners of a majority of the stock in a corporation.

Owners, Minority

Owners of a minority of the stock in a corporation.

Owners, Residual

Owners of instruments with junior claim in participation in dividends and against assets in the event of liquidation.

Pa-Pr

Par

In the case of a common share, par means a dollar amount assigned to the share by the company's charter. Par value also may be used to compute the dollar amount of the common shares or the balance sheet. Par value has little significance so far as market value of common stock is concerned. Many companies today issue no par stock, but give a stated per-share value on the balance sheet. Par at one time was supposed to represent the value of the original investment behind each share in cash, goods or services. In the case of preferred shares and bonds, however, par is important. It often signifies the dollar value upon which dividends on preferred stocks and interest on bonds, are figured. The issuer of a 3 percent bond promises to pay that percentage of the bond's par value annually. (See Capitalization.).

Partner

One of the owners of an incorporated business.

Partnership

An association of two or more persons co-owning a business for profit.

Patent

A right to a process or a product granted to its inventor or his assignee for his exclusive use.

Physical Inventory, Taking Of

Counting all merchandise on hand, usually at the end of an accounting period.

Preferred Stock

A class of stock with a claim on the company's earnings at a specified rate, before payment may be made on the common stock. Also usually entitled to priority over common stock if the company liquidates. Cumulative preferred stock has a provision that if one or more dividends are omitted, the omitted dividends must be paid before dividends may be paid on the company's common stock.

Present Value

The value in current dollars of a future sum.

Pr-R

Price-earnings ratio
Average market price of a company's stock divided by earnings per share.

Profit-and-Loss Statement Or Income Statement
A statement summarizing the income and expenses of a company to show net profit or loss for the period involved.

Profit, Gross
Sales minus cost of goods sold.

Promissory Note
A written promise to pay a sum of money at a specified future date.

Proprietor
The owner of an unincorporated business

Prorate
To spread equally over a period of time; allocate.

Redemption
The process of repaying the stockholders (or bondholders) of a corporation for their investments (or loans).

Residual Value
Estimated scrap value of a tangible asset.

Retained Earnings
Those profits kept in a corporation and not distributed as dividends.

Return On Stockholders' Investment
Net income divided by average owners' equity for the period.

Revenue
An increase in owners' equity arising from operations.

Se-St

Service Business

A firm dealing in non-merchandising activities.

Simple Interest

Interest on principal only as compared to compound interest which is interest on both principal and accumulated interest.

Sinking Fund

Money regularly set aside by a company to redeem its bonds or preferred stock from time to time as specified in the indenture or charter.

Social Security Tax

See FICA tax.

Sole Proprietorship

A business owned by one person.

Solvency

Ability to meet interest costs and repayment schedules associated with long-term obligations.

Stock, Authorized

The number of shares authorized by directors for issuance to investors.

Stock, Common

A residual share in the ownership of a corporation after liabilities and other property claims have been satisfied and entitling the owner to dividends and a vote in certain matters.

Stock Dividend

A dividend paid in securities rather than in cash; the dividend may be in additional shares of the issuing company or in shares of another company (usually a subsidiary) held by the company.

Stock, Preferred

A class of stock entitled to preferential treatment with regard to dividends or with regard to the distribution of assets in the event of liquidation.

St-T

Stockholder

The owners of an incorporated business, the ownership being evidenced by stock certificates.

Surplus

The excess of assets over creditor liabilities and capital stocks. When accumulated from profits, it is called retained earnings. If from other sources, it is called capital surplus, recapitalization surplus and so on. The sale of stock at prices above the par value results in paid-in-surplus equal to the excess of sale price over par value.

Surplus, Capital

An increase in owners' equity not generated through the company's earnings.

Surplus, Earned

Obsolete name for retained earnings.

Tangible Asset

A physical asset; a plant asset.

Taxable Income

Income on which income tax is computed: Gross income minus both exemptions and personal deductions.

Resources

••• Online Resources •••

◆ **About.com**

http://www.sbinformation.about.com

◆ **AltaVista Small Business**

*http://altavista.looksmart.com/eus1/eus65300/
eus65319/r?l&izf&*

◆ **America's Business Funding Directory**

http://www.business finance.com/search.asp

◆ **AOL.COM Business & Careers**

http://www.aol.com/webcenters/workplace/home.adp

◆ **BizMove.com**

http://www.bizmove.com

◆ **Biztalk.com Small Business Community**

http://www.biztalk.com

◆ **Bplans.com!**

http://www.bplans.com

◆ **BusinessTown.Com**
   http://www.businesstown.com

◆ **Council of Better Business Bureaus, Inc.**
   http://www.bbb.org

◆ **Education Index, Business Resources**
   http://www.educationindex.com/bus

◆ **Electric Library Business Edition**
   http://www.business.elibrary.com

◆ **EntrepreneurMag.com**
   http://www.entrepreneurmag.com

◆ **Federal Trade Commission-Franchise and Business Opportunities**
   http://www.ftc.gov/bcp/menu-fran.htm

◆ **HotBot Directory/Small Business**
   http://directory.hotbot.com/Business/Small_Business

◆ **Inc. Online**
   http://www.inc.com

◆ **Infoseek: Small Business**
   http://infoseek.go.com/Center/Business/Small_business

◆ **Internal Revenue Service**
   http://www.irs.ustreas.gov/prod/cover.html

◆ **International Finance & Commodities Institute**
   http://finance.wat.ch/IFCI

◆ **LNET-LLC-The Limited Liability Companies and Partnerships Conference**
   http://www.stcl.edu/lnet-llc/lnet-llc.html

◆ **Limited Liability Company Website**
   http://www.llcweb.com

- **Lycos Directory: Small Business**
  http://dir.lycos.com/Business/Small_Business

- **Netscape Women in Business**
  http://women.netscape.com/smallbusiness

- **National Association of Small Business Investment Companies**
  http://www.nasbic.org

- **National Foundation for Women Business Owners (NFWBO)**
  http://www.nfwbo.org

- **National Small Business Development Center (SBDC) Research Network**
  http://www.smallbiz.suny.edu

- **National Small Business Network Resource Directory**
  http://businessknowhow.net/Directory/bkhDindex.asp

- **National Small Business United**
  http://www.nsbu.org

- **North American Securities Administrators Association (NASAA)**
  http://www.nasaa.org

- **Occupational Safety and Health Administration (OSHA)**
  http://www.osha.gov

- **Service Core of Retired Executives**
  http://www.score.org

- **Small Business Advisor**
  http://www.isquare.com

- **Small Business Assistance, Environmental Protection Agency**
  http://es.epa.gov/new/business/business.html

◆ **Small Business Innovation Research (SBIR) Program**
   http://es.epa.gov/business/index.html

◆ **Small Business Primer**
   http://www.ces.ncsu.edu/depts/fcs/business/welcome.html

◆ **Small Business Resource**
   http://www.irl.co.uk/sbr

◆ **Small Business Taxes & Management**
   http://www.smbiz.com

◆ **Smalloffice.com**
   http://www.smalloffice.com

◆ **Tax and Accounting Sites Directory**
   http://www.taxsites.com

◆ **U.S. Business Advisor**
   http://www.business.gov

◆ **U.S. Chamber of Commerce**
   http://www.uschamber.org/smallbiz/index.html

◆ **U.S. Equal Employment Opportunity Commission's (EEOC)**
   http://www.eeoc.gov

◆ **U.S. Government Printing Office-Small Business**
   http://www.access.gpo.gov/su_docs/sale/sb-307.html

◆ **U.S. Small Business Administration**
   http://www.sbaonline.sba.gov

◆ **U.S. Treasury Department-Business Services**
   http://www.ustreas.gov/busserv.html

◆ **Webcrawler: Small Business**
   http://quicken.webcrawler.com/small_business

◆ **Yahoo! Business and Economy: Marketing**
http://dir.yahoo.com/Business_and_Economy/Marketing

◆ **Yahoo! Small Business**
http://smallbusiness.yahoo.com

••• Legal Search Engines •••

◆ **All Law**
http://www.alllaw.com

◆ **American Law Sources On Line**
http://www.lawsource.com/also/searchfm.htm

◆ **Catalaw**
http://www.catalaw.com

◆ **FindLaw**
http://www.findlaw.com

◆ **InternetOracle**
http://www.internetoracle.com/legal.htm

◆ **LawAid**
http://www.lawaid.com/search.html

◆ **LawCrawler**
http://www.lawcrawler.com

◆ **LawEngine, The**
http://www.fastsearch.com/law

◆ **LawRunner**
http://www.lawrunner.com

◆ **'Lectric Law Library™**
http://www.lectlaw.com

- **Legal Search Engines**

  http://www.dreamscape.com/frankvad/search.legal.html

- **LEXIS/NEXIS Communications Center**

  http://www.lexis-nexis.com/lncc/general/search.html

- **Meta-Index for U.S. Legal Research**

  http://gsulaw.gsu.edu/metaindex

- **Seamless Website, The**

  http://seamless.com

- **USALaw**

  http://www.usalaw.com/linksrch.cfm

- **WestLaw**

  http://westdoc.com (Registered users only. Fee paid service.)

••• State Bar Associations •••

ALABAMA

Alabama State Bar
415 Dexter Avenue
Montgomery, AL 36104

mailing address:
PO Box 671
Montgomery, AL 36101
(334) 269-1515

http://www.alabar.org

ALASKA

Alaska Bar Association
510 L Street No. 602
Anchorage, AK 99501

mailing address:
PO Box 100279
Anchorage, AK 99510

ARIZONA

State Bar of Arizona
111 West Monroe
Phoenix, AZ 85003-1742
(602) 252-4804

ARKANSAS

Arkansas Bar Association
400 West Markham
Little Rock, AR 72201
(501) 375-4605

CALIFORNIA

State Bar of California
555 Franklin Street
San Francisco, CA 94102
(415) 561-8200

http://www.calbar.org
Alameda County Bar
Association

http://www.acbanet.org

COLORADO
Colorado Bar Association
No. 950, 1900 Grant Street
Denver, CO 80203
(303) 860-1115

http://www.cobar.org

CONNECTICUT
Connecticut Bar Association
101 Corporate Place
Rocky Hill, CT 06067-1894
(203) 721-0025

DELAWARE
Delaware State Bar Association
1225 King Street, 10th floor
Wilmington, DE 19801
(302) 658-5279
(302) 658-5278 (lawyer referral service)

DISTRICT OF COLUMBIA
District of Columbia Bar
1250 H Street, NW, 6th Floor
Washington, DC 20005
(202) 737-4700

Bar Association of the District of Columbia
1819 H Street, NW, 12th floor
Washington, DC 20006-3690
(202) 223-6600

FLORIDA
The Florida Bar
The Florida Bar Center
650 Apalachee Parkway
Tallahassee, FL 32399-2300
(850) 561-5600

GEORGIA
State Bar of Georgia
800 The Hurt Building
50 Hurt Plaza
Atlanta, GA 30303
(404) 527-8700

http://www.gabar.org

HAWAII
Hawaii State Bar Association
1136 Union Mall
Penthouse 1
Honolulu, HI 96813
(808) 537-1868

http://www.hsba.org

IDAHO
Idaho State Bar
PO Box 895
Boise, ID 83701
(208) 334-4500

ILLINOIS
Illinois State Bar Association
424 South Second Street
Springfield, IL 62701
(217) 525-1760

INDIANA
Indiana State Bar Association
230 East Ohio Street
Indianapolis, IN 46204
(317) 639-5465

http://www.iquest.net/isba

IOWA
Iowa State Bar Association
521 East Locust
Des Moines, IA 50309
(515) 243-3179

http://www.iowabar.org

KANSAS
Kansas Bar Association
1200 Harrison Street
Topeka, KS 66601
(913) 234-5696

http://www.ink.org/public/ cybar

KENTUCKY
Kentucky Bar Association
514 West Main Street
Frankfort, KY 40601-1883
(502) 564-3795

http://www.kybar.org

LOUISIANA
Louisiana State Bar Association
601 St. Charles Avenue
New Orleans, LA 70130
(504) 566-1600

MAINE
Maine State Bar Association
124 State Street
PO Box 788
Augusta, ME 04330
(207) 622-7523

http://www.mainebar.org

MARYLAND
Maryland State Bar Association
520 West Fayette Street
Baltimore, MD 21201
(301) 685-7878

http://www.msba.org/msba

MASSACHUSETTS
Massachusetts Bar Association
20 West Street
Boston, MA 02111
(617) 542-3602
(617) 542-9103 (lawyer referral service)

MICHIGAN
State Bar of Michigan
306 Townsend Street
Lansing, MI 48933-2083
(517) 372-9030

http://www.michbar.org

MINNESOTA
Minnesota State Bar Association
514 Nicollet Mall
Minneapolis, MN 55402
(612) 333-1183

MISSISSIPPI
The Mississippi Bar
643 No. State Street
Jackson, Mississippi 39202
(601) 948-4471

MISSOURI
The Missouri Bar
P.O. Box 119, 326 Monroe
Jefferson City, Missouri 65102
(314) 635-4128

http://www.mobar.org

MONTANA
State Bar of Montana
46 North Main
PO Box 577
Helena, MT 59624
(406) 442-7660

NEBRASKA
Nebraska State Bar Association
635 South 14th Street, 2nd floor
Lincoln, NE 68508
(402) 475-7091

http://www.nebar.com

NEVADA
State Bar of Nevada
201 Las Vegas Blvd.
Las Vegas, NV 89101
(702) 382-2200

http://www.nvbar.org

NEW HAMPSHIRE
New Hampshire Bar Association
112 Pleasant Street
Concord, NH 03301
(603) 224-6942

NEW JERSEY
New Jersey State Bar Association
One Constitution Square
New Brunswick, NJ 08901-1500
(908) 249-5000

NEW MEXICO
State Bar of New Mexico
121 Tijeras Street N.E.
Albuquerque, NM 87102

mailing address:
PO Box 25883
Albuquerque, NM 87125
(505) 843-6132

NEW YORK
New York State Bar Association
One Elk Street
Albany, NY 12207
(518) 463-3200

http://www.nysba.org

NORTH CAROLINA
North Carolina State Bar
208 Fayetteville Street Mall
Raleigh, NC 27601

mailing address:
PO Box 25908
Raleigh, NC 27611
(919) 828-4620

North Carolina Bar Association
1312 Annapolis Drive
Raleigh, NC 27608

mailing address:
PO Box 12806
Raleigh, NC 27605
(919) 828-0561

http://www.barlinc.org

NORTH DAKOTA
State Bar Association of North
Dakota
515 1/2 East Broadway, suite 101
Bismarck, ND 58501

mailing address:
PO Box 2136
Bismarck, ND 58502
(701) 255-1404

OHIO
Ohio State Bar Association
1700 Lake Shore Drive
Columbus, OH 43204

mailing address:
PO Box 16562
Columbus, OH 43216-6562
(614) 487-2050

OKLAHOMA
Oklahoma Bar Association
1901 North Lincoln
Oklahoma City, OK 73105
(405) 524-2365

OREGON
Oregon State Bar
5200 S.W. Meadows Road
PO Box 1689
Lake Oswego, OR 97035-0889
(503) 620-0222

PENNSYLVANIA
Pennsylvania Bar Association
100 South Street
PO Box 186
Harrisburg, PA 17108
(717) 238-6715

Pennsylvania Bar Institute
http://www.pbi.org

PUERTO RICO
Puerto Rico Bar Association
PO Box 1900
San Juan, Puerto Rico 00903
(787) 721-3358

RHODE ISLAND
Rhode Island Bar Association
115 Cedar Street
Providence, RI 02903
(401) 421-5740

SOUTH CAROLINA
South Carolina Bar
950 Taylor Street
PO Box 608
Columbia, SC 29202
(803) 799-6653

http://www.scbar.org

SOUTH DAKOTA
State Bar of South Dakota
222 East Capitol
Pierre, SD 57501
(605) 224-7554

TENNESSEE
Tennessee Bar Assn
3622 West End Avenue
Nashville, TN 37205
(615) 383-7421

http://www.tba.org

TEXAS
State Bar of Texas
1414 Colorado
PO Box 12487
Austin, TX 78711
(512) 463-1463

UTAH
Utah State Bar
645 South 200 East, Suite 310
Salt Lake City, UT 84111
(801) 531-9077

VERMONT
Vermont Bar Association
PO Box 100
Montpelier, VT 05601
(802) 223-2020

VIRGINIA
Virginia State Bar
707 East Main Street, suite 1500
Richmond, VA 23219-0501
(804) 775-0500

Virginia Bar Association
701 East Franklin St., Suite 1120
Richmond, VA 23219
(804) 644-0041

VIRGIN ISLANDS
Virgin Islands Bar Association
P.O. Box 4108
Christiansted, Virgin Islands
00822
(340) 778-7497

WASHINGTON
Washington State Bar Association
500 Westin Street
2001 Sixth Avenue
Seattle, WA 98121-2599
(206) 727-8200

http://www.wsba.org

WEST VIRGINIA
West Virginia State Bar
2006 Kanawha Blvd. East
Charleston, WV 25311
(304) 558-2456

http://www.wvbar.org

West Virginia Bar Association
904 Security Building
100 Capitol Street
Charleston, WV 25301
(304) 342-1474

WISCONSIN
State Bar of Wisconsin
402 West Wilson Street
Madison, WI 53703
(608) 257-3838

*http://www.wisbar.org/
home.htm*

WYOMING
Wyoming State Bar
500 Randall Avenue
Cheyenne, WY 82001
PO Box 109
Cheyenne, WY 82003
(307) 632-9061

How to save on attorney fees

How to save on attorney fees

Millions of Americans know they need legal protection, whether it's to get agreements in writing, protect themselves from lawsuits, or document business transactions. But too often these basic but important legal matters are neglected because of something else millions of Americans know: legal services are expensive.

They don't have to be. In response to the demand for affordable legal protection and services, there are now specialized clinics that process simple documents. Paralegals help people prepare legal claims on a freelance basis. People find they can handle their own legal affairs with do-it-yourself legal guides and kits. Indeed, this book is a part of this growing trend.

When are these alternatives to a lawyer appropriate? If you hire an attorney, how can you make sure you're getting good advice for a reasonable fee? Most importantly, do you know how to lower your legal expenses?

When there is no alternative

Make no mistake: serious legal matters require a lawyer. The tips in this book can help you reduce your legal fees, but there is no alternative to good professional legal services in certain circumstances:

- when you are charged with a felony, you are a repeat offender, or jail is possible

- when a substantial amount of money or property is at stake in a lawsuit

- when you are a party in an adversarial divorce or custody case

- when you are an alien facing deportation

- when you are the plaintiff in a personal injury suit that involves large sums of money

- when you're involved in very important transactions

Are you sure you want to take it to court?

Consider the following questions before you pursue legal action:

What are your financial resources?

Money buys experienced attorneys, and experience wins over first-year lawyers and public defenders. Even with a strong case, you may save money by not going to court. Yes, people win millions in court. But for every big winner there are ten plaintiffs who either lose or win so little that litigation wasn't worth their effort.

Do you have the time and energy for a trial?

Courts are overbooked, and by the time your case is heard your initial zeal may have grown cold. If you can, make a reasonable settlement out of court. On personal matters, like a divorce or custody case, consider the emotional toll on all parties. Any legal case will affect you in some way. You will need time away from work. A newsworthy case may bring press coverage. Your loved ones, too, may face publicity. There is usually good reason to settle most cases quickly, quietly, and economically.

How can you settle disputes without litigation?

Consider *mediation*. In mediation, each party pays half the mediator's fee and, together, they attempt to work out a compromise informally. *Binding arbitration* is another alternative. For a small fee, a trained specialist serves as judge, hears both sides, and hands down a ruling that both parties have agreed to accept.

So you need an attorney

Having done your best to avoid litigation, if you still find yourself headed for court, you will need an attorney. To get the right attorney at a reasonable cost, be guided by these four questions:

What type of case is it?

You don't seek a foot doctor for a toothache. Find an attorney experienced in your type of legal problem. If you can get recommendations from clients who have recently won similar cases, do so.

Where will the trial be held?

You want a lawyer familiar with that court system and one who knows the court personnel and the local protocol—which can vary from one locality to another.

Should you hire a large or small firm?

Hiring a senior partner at a large and prestigious law firm sounds reassuring, but chances are the actual work will be handled by associates—at high rates. Small firms may give your case more attention but, with fewer resources, take longer to get the work done.

What can you afford?

Hire an attorney you can afford, of course, but know what a fee quote includes. High fees may reflect a firm's luxurious offices, high-paid staff and unmonitored expenses, while low estimates may mean "unexpected" costs later. Ask for a written estimate of all costs and anticipated expenses.

How to find a good lawyer

Whether you need an attorney quickly or you're simply open to future possibilities, here are seven nontraditional methods for finding your lawyer:

1) **Word of mouth**: Successful lawyers develop reputations. Your friends, business associates and other professionals are potential referral sources. But beware of hiring a friend. Keep the client-attorney relationship strictly business.

2) **Directories**: The Yellow Pages and the Martin-Hubbell Lawyer Directory (in your local library) can help you locate a lawyer with the right education, background and expertise for your case.

3) **Databases**: A paralegal should be able to run a quick computer search of local attorneys for you using the Westlaw or Lexis database.

4) **State bar associations**: Bar associations are listed in phone books. Along with lawyer referrals, your bar association can direct you to low-cost legal clinics or specialists in your area.

5) **Law schools**: Did you know that a legal clinic run by a law school gives law students hands-on experience? This may fit your legal needs. A third-year law student loaded with enthusiasm and a little experience might fill the bill quite inexpensively—or even for free.

6) **Advertisements**: Ads are a lawyer's business card. If a "TV attorney" seems to have a good track record with your kind of case, why not call? Just don't be swayed by the glamour of a high-profile attorney.

7) **Your own ad**: A small ad describing the qualifications and legal expertise you're seeking, placed in a local bar association journal, may get you just the lead you need.

How to hire and work with your attorney

No matter how you hear about an attorney, you must interview him or her in person. Call the office during business hours and ask to speak to the attorney directly. Then explain your case briefly and mention how you obtained the attorney's name. If the attorney sounds interested and knowledgeable, arrange for a visit.

The ten-point visit

1) Note the address. This is a good indication of the rates to expect.

2) Note the condition of the offices. File-laden desks and poorly maintained work space may indicate a poorly run firm.

3) Look for up-to-date computer equipment and an adequate complement of support personnel.

4) Note the appearance of the attorney. How will he or she impress a judge or jury?

5) Is the attorney attentive? Does the attorney take notes, ask questions, follow up on points you've mentioned?

6)   Ask what schools he or she has graduated from, and feel free to check credentials with the state bar association.

7)   Does the attorney have a good track record with your type of case?

8)   Does he or she explain legal terms to you in plain English?

9)   Are the firm's costs reasonable?

10) Will the attorney provide references?

Hiring the attorney

Having chosen your attorney, make sure all the terms are agreeable. Send letters to any other attorneys you have interviewed, thanking them for their time and interest in your case and explaining that you have retained another attorney's services.

Request a letter from your new attorney outlining your retainer agreement. The letter should list all fees you will be responsible for as well as the billing arrangement. Did you arrange to pay in installments? This should be noted in your retainer agreement.

Controlling legal costs

Legal fees and expenses can get out of control easily, but the client who is willing to put in the effort can keep legal costs manageable. Work out a budget with your attorney. Create a timeline for your case. Estimate the costs involved in each step.

Legal fees can be straightforward. Some lawyers charge a fixed rate for a specific project. Others charge contingency fees (they collect a percentage of your recovery, usually 35-50 percent if you win and nothing if you lose). But most attorneys prefer to bill by the hour. Expenses can run the gamut, with one hourly charge for taking depositions and another for making copies.

Have your attorney give you a list of charges for services rendered and an itemized monthly bill. The bill should explain the service performed, who performed the work, when the service was provided, how long it took, and how the service benefits your case.

Ample opportunity abounds in legal billing for dishonesty and greed. There is also plenty of opportunity for knowledgeable clients to cut their bills significantly if they know what to look for. Asking the right questions and setting limits on fees is smart and can save you a bundle. Don't be afraid to question legal bills. It's your case and your money!

When the bill arrives

- **Retainer fees**: You should already have a written retainer agreement. Ideally, the retainer fee applies toward case costs, and your agreement puts that in writing. Protect yourself by escrowing the retainer fee until the case has been handled to your satisfaction.

- **Office visit charges**: Track your case and all documents, correspondence, and bills. Diary all dates, deadlines and questions you want to ask your attorney during your next office visit. This keeps expensive office visits focused and productive, with more accomplished in less time. If your attorney charges less for phone consultations than office visits, reserve visits for those tasks that must be done in person.

- **Phone bills**: This is where itemized bills are essential. Who made the call, who was spoken to, what was discussed, when was the call made, and how long did it last? Question any charges that seem unnecessary or excessive (over 60 minutes).

- **Administrative costs**: Your case may involve hundreds, if not thousands, of documents: motions, affidavits, depositions, interrogatories, bills, memoranda, and letters. Are they all necessary? Understand your attorney's case strategy before paying for an endless stream of costly documents.

- **Associate and paralegal fees**: Note in your retainer agreement which staff people will have access to your file. Then you'll have an informed and efficient staff working on your case, and you'll recognize their names on your bill. Of course, your attorney should handle the important part of your case, but less costly paralegals or associates may handle routine matters more economically. Note: Some firms expect their associates to meet a quota of billable hours, although the time spent is not always warranted. Review your bill. Does the time spent make sense for the document in question? Are several staff involved in matters that should be handled by one person? Don't be afraid to ask questions. And withhold payment until you have satisfactory answers.

- **Court stenographer fees**: Depositions and court hearings require costly transcripts and stenographers. This means added expenses. Keep an eye on these costs.

- **Copying charges**: Your retainer fee should limit the number of copies made of your complete file. This is in your legal interest, because multiple files mean multiple chances others may access your confidential information. It is also in your financial interest, because copying costs can be astronomical.

- **Fax costs**: As with the phone and copier, the fax can easily run up costs. Set a limit.

- **Postage charges**: Be aware of how much it costs to send a legal document overnight, or a registered letter. Offer to pick up or deliver expensive items when it makes sense.

- **Filing fees**: Make it clear to your attorney that you want to minimize the number of court filings in your case. Watch your bill and question any filing that seems unnecessary.

- **Document production fee**: Turning over documents to your opponent is mandatory and expensive. If you're faced with reproducing boxes of documents, consider having the job done by a commercial firm rather than your attorney's office.

- **Research and investigations**: Pay only for photographs that can be used in court. Can you hire a photographer at a lower rate than what your attorney charges? Reserve that right in your retainer agreement. Database research can also be extensive and expensive; if your attorney uses Westlaw or Nexis, set limits on the research you will pay for.

- **Expert witnesses**: Question your attorney if you are expected to pay for more than a reasonable number of expert witnesses. Limit the number to what is essential to your case.

- **Technology costs**: Avoid videos, tape recordings, and graphics if you can use old-fashioned diagrams to illustrate your case.

- **Travel expenses**: Travel expenses for those connected to your case can be quite costly unless you set a maximum budget. Check all travel-related items on your bill, and make sure they are appropriate. Always question why the travel is necessary before you agree to pay for it.

- **Appeals costs**: Losing a case often means an appeal, but weigh the costs involved before you make that decision. If money is at stake, do a cost-benefit analysis to see if an appeal is financially justified.

- **Monetary damages**: Your attorney should be able to help you estimate the total damages you will have to pay if you lose a civil case. Always consider settling out of court rather than proceeding to trial when the trial costs will be high.

- **Surprise costs**: Surprise costs are so routine they're predictable. The judge may impose unexpected court orders on one or both sides, or the opposition will file an unexpected motion that increases your legal costs. Budget a few thousand dollars over what you estimate your case will cost. It usually is needed.

- **Padded expenses**: Assume your costs and expenses are legitimate. But some firms do inflate expenses—office supplies, database searches, copying, postage, phone bills—to bolster their bottom line. Request copies of bills your law firm receives from support services. If you are not the only client represented on a bill, determine those charges related to your case.

Keeping it legal without a lawyer

The best way to save legal costs is to avoid legal problems. There are hundreds of ways to decrease your chances of lawsuits and other nasty legal encounters. Most simply involve a little common sense. You can also use your own initiative to find and use the variety of self-help legal aid available to consumers.

11 situations in which you may not need a lawyer

1) **No-fault divorce**: Married couples with no children, minimal property, and no demands for alimony can take advantage of divorce mediation services. A lawyer should review your divorce agreement before you sign it, but you will have saved a fortune in attorney fees. A marital or family counselor may save a seemingly doomed marriage, or help both parties move beyond anger to a calm settlement. Either way, counseling can save you money.

2) **Wills**: Do-it-yourself wills and living trusts are ideal for people with estates of less than $600,000. Even if an attorney reviews your final documents, a will kit allows you to read the documents, ponder your bequests, fill out sample forms, and discuss your wishes with your family at your leisure, without a lawyer's meter running.

3) **Incorporating**: Incorporating a small business can be done by any business owner. Your state government office provides the forms and instructions necessary. A visit to your state office will probably be

necessary to perform a business name check. A fee of $100-$200 is usually charged for processing your Articles of Incorporation. The rest is paperwork: filling out forms correctly; holding regular, official meetings; and maintaining accurate records.

4) **Routine business transactions**: Copyrights, for example, can be applied for by asking the U.S. Copyright Office for the appropriate forms and brochures. The same is true of the U.S. Patent and Trademark Office. If your business does a great deal of document preparation and research, hire a certified paralegal rather than paying an attorney's rates. Consider mediation or binding arbitration rather than going to court for a business dispute. Hire a human resources/benefits administrator to head off disputes concerning discrimination or other employee charges.

5) **Repairing bad credit**: When money matters get out of hand, attorneys and bankruptcy should not be your first solution. Contact a credit counseling organization that will help you work out manageable payment plans so that everyone wins. It can also help you learn to manage your money better. A good company to start with is the Consumer Credit Counseling Service, 1-800-388-2227.

6) **Small Claims Court**: For legal grievances amounting to a few thousand dollars in damages, represent yourself in Small Claims Court. There is a small filing fee, forms to fill out, and several court visits necessary. If you can collect evidence, state your case in a clear and logical presentation, and come across as neat, respectful and sincere, you can succeed in Small Claims Court.

7) **Traffic Court**: Like Small Claims Court, Traffic Court may show more compassion to a defendant appearing without an attorney. If you are ticketed for a minor offense and want to take it to court, you will be asked to plead guilty or not guilty. If you plead guilty, you can ask for leniency in sentencing by presenting mitigating circumstances. Bring any witnesses who can support your story, and remember that presentation (some would call it acting ability) is as important as fact.

8) **Residential zoning petition**: If a homeowner wants to open a home business, build an addition, or make other changes that may affect his or her neighborhood, town approval is required. But you don't need a lawyer to fill out a zoning variance application, turn it in, and present your story at a public hearing. Getting local support before the hearing is the best way to assure a positive vote; contact as many neighbors as possible to reassure them that your plans won't adversely affect them or the neighborhood.

9) **Government benefit applications**: Applying for veterans' or unemployment benefits may be daunting, but the process doesn't require legal help. Apply for either immediately upon becoming eligible. Note: If your former employer contests your application for unemployment benefits and you have to defend yourself at a hearing, you may want to consider hiring an attorney.

10) **Receiving government files**: The Freedom of Information Act gives every American the right to receive copies of government information about him or her. Write a letter to the appropriate state or federal agency, noting the precise information you want. List each document in a separate paragraph. Mention the Freedom of Information Act, and state that you will pay any expenses. Close with your signature and the address the documents should be sent to. An approved request may take six months to arrive. If it is refused on the grounds that the information is classified or violates another's privacy, send a letter of appeal explaining why the released information would not endanger anyone. Enlist the support of your local state or federal representative, if possible, to smooth the approval process.

11) **Citizenship**: Arriving in the United States to work and become a citizen is a process tangled in bureaucratic red tape, but it requires more perseverance than legal assistance. Immigrants can learn how to obtain a "Green Card," under what circumstances they can work, and what the requirements of citizenship are by contacting the Immigration Services or reading a good self-help book.

Save more; it's E-Z

When it comes to saving attorneys' fees, Made E-Z Products is the consumer's best friend. America's largest publisher of self-help legal products offers legally valid forms for virtually every situation. E-Z Legal Kits and Made E-Z Guides covering legal topics include all necessary forms with a simple-to-follow manual of instructions or a layman's book. Made E-Z Books are a library of forms and documents for everyday business and personal needs. Made E-Z Software provides those same forms on disk and CD for customized documents at the touch of the keyboard.

You can add to your legal savvy and your ability to protect yourself, your loved ones, your business and your property with a range of self-help legal titles available through Made E-Z Products.

Save On Legal Fees

Fast answers to 90%
of your legal questions

Clear, reliable & up-to-date

Save costly legal fees
& protect your rights

More than a reference...
a complete do-it-yourself tool!

Stock No.: BK311
$29.95 8.5" x 11"
500 pages Soft cover
ISBN 1-56382-311-X

Everyday Law Made E-Z

The book that saves legal fees every time it's opened.

Here, in *Everyday Law Made E-Z*, are fast answers to 90% of the legal
questions anyone is ever likely to ask, such as:

- How can I control my neighbor's pet?
- Can I change my name?
- What is a common law marriage?
- When should I incorporate my business?
- Is a child responsible for his bills?
- Who owns a husband's gifts to his wife?
- How do I become a naturalized citizen?
- Should I get my divorce in Nevada?
- Can I write my own will?
- Who is responsible when my son drives my car?
- How can my uncle get a Green Card?
- What are the rights of a non-smoker?
- Do I have to let the police search my car?
- What is sexual harassment?
- When is euthanasia legal?
- What repairs must my landlord make?
- What's the difference between fair criticism and slander?
- When can I get my deposit back?
- Can I sue the federal government?
- Am I responsible for a drunken guest's auto accident?
- Is a hotel liable if it does not honor a reservation?
- Does my car fit the lemon law?

Whether for personal or business use, this 500-page information-packed book
helps the layman safeguard his property, avoid disputes, comply with legal
obligations, and enforce his rights. Hundreds of cases illustrate thousands of
points of law, each clearly and completely explained.

MADE E-Z
PRODUCTS

Whatever you need to know, we've made it E-Z!

Informative text and forms you can fill out on-screen.* From personal to business, legal to leisure—we've made it E-Z!

PERSONAL & FAMILY

For all your family's needs, we have titles that will help keep you organized and guide you through most every aspect of your personal life.

BUSINESS

Whether you're starting from scratch with a home business or you just want to keep your corporate records in shape, we've got the programs for you.

	Item#	Qty.	Price Ea.†
★ **E✦Z Legal Kits**			
Bankruptcy	K100		$23.95
Incorporation	K101		$23.95
Divorce	K102		$29.95
Credit Repair	K103		$21.95
Living Trust	K105		$21.95
Living Will	K106		$23.95
Last Will & Testament	K107		$18.95
Buying/Selling Your Home	K111		$21.95
Employment Law	K112		$21.95
Collecting Child Support	K115		$21.95
Limited Liability Company	K116		$21.95
★ **Made E✦Z Software**			
Accounting Made E-Z	SW1207		$29.95
Asset Protection Made E-Z	SW1157		$29.95
Bankruptcy Made E-Z	SW1154		$29.95
Best Career Oppportunities Made E-Z	SW1216		$29.95
Brain-Buster Crossword Puzzles	SW1223		$29.95
Brain-Buster Jigsaw Puzzles	SW1222		$29.95
Business Startups Made E-Z	SW1192		$29.95
Buying/Selling Your Home Made E-Z	SW1213		$29.95
Car Buying Made E-Z	SW1146		$29.95
Corporate Record Keeping Made E-Z	SW1159		$29.95
Credit Repair Made E-Z	SW1153		$29.95
Divorce Law Made E-Z	SW1182		$29.95
Everyday Law Made E-Z	SW1185		$29.95
Everyday Legal Forms & Agreements	SW1186		$29.95
Incorporation Made E-Z	SW1176		$29.95
Last Wills Made E-Z	SW1177		$29.95
Living Trusts Made E-Z	SW1178		$29.95
Offshore Investing Made E-Z	SW1218		$29.95
Owning a Franchise Made E-Z	SW1202		$29.95
Touring Florence, Italy Made E-Z	SW1220		$29.95
Touring London, England Made E-Z	SW1221		$29.95
Vital Record Keeping Made E-Z	SW1160		$29.95
Website Marketing Made E-Z	SW1203		$29.95
Your Profitable Home Business	SW1204		$29.95
★ **Made E✦Z Guides**			
Bankruptcy Made E-Z	G200		$17.95
Incorporation Made E-Z	G201		$17.95
Divorce Law Made E-Z	G202		$17.95
Credit Repair Made E-Z	G203		$17.95
Living Trusts Made E-Z	G205		$17.95
Living Wills Made E-Z	G206		$17.95
Last Wills Made E-Z	G207		$17.95
Small Claims Court Made E-Z	G209		$17.95
Traffic Court Made E-Z	G210		$17.95
Buying/Selling Your Home Made E-Z	G211		$17.95
Employment Law Made E-Z	G212		$17.95
Collecting Child Support Made E-Z	G215		$17.95
Limited Liability Companies Made E-Z	G216		$17.95
Partnerships Made E-Z	G218		$17.95
Solving IRS Problems Made E-Z	G219		$17.95
Asset Protection Secrets Made E-Z	G220		$17.95
Immigration Made E-Z	G223		$17.95
Buying/Selling a Business Made E-Z	G223		$17.95
★ **Made E✦Z Books**			
Managing Employees Made E-Z	BK308		$29.95
Corporate Record Keeping Made E-Z	BK310		$29.95
Vital Record Keeping Made E-Z	BK312		$29.95
Business Forms Made E-Z	BK313		$29.95
Collecting Unpaid Bills Made E-Z	BK309		$29.95
Everyday Law Made E-Z	BK311		$29.95
Everyday Legal Forms & Agreements	BK307		$29.95
★ **Labor Posters**			
Federal Labor Law Poster	LP001		$11.99
State Labor Law Poster (specify state)			$29.95
★ SHIPPING & HANDLING*			$
★ **TOTAL OF ORDER**:			$

ss 1999.r2

See an item in this book you would like to order?

To order :
1. Photocopy this order form.
2. Use the photocopy to complete your order and mail to:

MADE E-Z PRODUCTS

384 S Military Trail, Deerfield Beach, FL 33442
phone: (954) 480-8933 • fax: (954) 480-8906
web site: http://www.e-zlegal.com/

†Prices current as of 10/99

Shipping and Handling: Add $3.50 for the first item, $1.50 for each additional item.

**Florida residents add 6% sales tax.

Total payment must accompany all orders.
Make checks payable to: Made E-Z Products, Inc.

NAME

COMPANY

ORGANIZATION

ADDRESS

CITY   STATE   ZIP

PHONE (   )

PAYMENT:

❑ CHECK ENCLOSED, PAYABLE TO MADE E-Z PRODUCTS, INC.

❑ PLEASE CHARGE MY ACCOUNT: ❑ MasterCard ❑ VISA

EXP. DATE

ACCOUNT NO.

Signature: _____
(required for credit card purchases)

-OR-

For faster service, order by phone:
(954) 480-8933

Or you can fax your order to us:
(954) 480-8906

Index